Inside NETBIOS

J. Scott Haugdahl
Architecture Technology Corporation

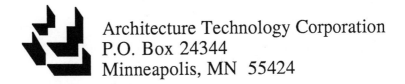

Architecture Technology Corporation
P.O. Box 24344
Minneapolis, MN 55424

Architecture Technology Corporation
P.O. Box 24344
Minneapolis, MN 55424

Library of Congress Cataloging in Publication Data Pending

ISBN 0-939405-01-6

Table of Contents

Chapter 6 - Microsoft Networks

List of Figures

DISCLAIMER

Architecture Technology Corporation makes no representations or warranties with respect to the contents hereof and specifically disclaims any implied warranties of merchantability or fitness for any particular purpose.

Further, reasonable care has been taken to ensure the accuracy of the book, but errors and omissions could have occurred. Architecture Technology assumes no responsibility for any incidental or consequential damages caused thereby.

Further, Architecture Technology Corporation reserves the right to revise this book and to make changes from time to time in the content thereof without obligation to notify any person or organization of such revision or changes.

This disclaimer applies to all parts of this book.

FOREWORD

Since 1981, Architecture Technology Corporation has gathered and disseminated information on computer architecture and PC LANs. The company's activities have included providing consulting and seminars and publishing newsletters, handbooks, and reports. *Inside NETBIOS*, by J. Scott Haugdahl, is the second in a series of books covering specific, timely topics in the field of LANs.

Inside NETBIOS is an in-depth monograph delving into NETBIOS and related technology issues. This very readable book begins with a history and conceptual view of NETBIOS and its relationship to the OSI Reference Model, continues with the command and packet structure of NETBIOS, details the server message block (SMB) protocols that rely on NETBIOS, and closes with a look at NETBIOS offerings from other vendors and the commonality between NETBIOS and MS Networks. *Inside NETBIOS* is essential reading for managers, implementors, and serious users of PC local area networks.

Architecture Technology Corporation

PREFACE

Network Basic Input/Output System (NETBIOS), a high-level programming interface to IBM LANs, was originally developed by Sytek, Inc., for IBM's IBM PC Network. IBM reiterated the importance of NETBIOS by offering a NETBIOS emulator with the Token-Ring.

Inside NETBIOS is a sequel to my previous book, *Inside the Token-Ring*. It is intended to give readers a more in-depth understanding of NETBIOS than the coverage offered by *Inside the Token-Ring*. Written to be beneficial to both technical and non- technical readers, this book includes general and overview information in addition to programming and design information.

Inside NETBIOS would not have been possible without the support I have received over the past five years from Architecture Technology and from many of my friends at a number of LAN companies as I have been actively researching, consulting, and presenting seminars on PC LAN-related matters.

J. Scott Haugdahl
Minneapolis, Minnesota
July 1986

To My Parents

Chapter 1 - Introduction

A brief history of the development of NETBIOS
A working definition of protocols
The OSI Reference Model
Communication between OSI layers
How NETBIOS relates to PC-DOS and applications
A general description of the NETBIOS protocol layers

1.1 History

Network Basic Input/Output System (NETBIOS), a high-level programming interface to IBM LANs, was originally developed by Sytek, Inc., for IBM's IBM PC Network. IBM reiterated the importance of NETBIOS by offering a NETBIOS emulator with the Token-Ring. This allows applications originally developed for the PC Network to be run on the Token-Ring.

Since NETBIOS is backed by IBM, many developers of LAN software and hardware are hoping that NETBIOS in conjunction with DOS 3.1/3.2 will develop into a standard interface for PC LANs and stop the proliferation of proprietary interfaces and protocols. DOS 3.1 or greater is required for the PC Network; DOS 3.2 or greater is required for the Token-Ring. In the past, vendors have had to write proprietary software or use published protocols such as Xerox Network Systems (XNS) or ARPANET-developed Transmission Control Protocol, Internetwork Protocol (TCP/IP) that have not yet been widely implemented in the PC LAN industry. In fact, NETBIOS would not have become a "de facto" standard for PC LANs if it had not been offered by IBM. Since NETBIOS was designed as an open interface in IBM's PC Network, it gave developers a thread of hope for standardization, at least at the session level interface (Layer 5 of the Open Systems Interconnect (OSI) model discussed later). NETBIOS certainly is influencing offerings from many independent (non-IBM) LAN vendors: most of them offer NETBIOS emulation.

1.2 A Working Definition of Protocols

Protocols are simply a set of conventions that allow two or more end points to communicate. There are essentially three elements in protocols: syntax, semantics, and timing. The syntax of a protocol defines the fields; for example, there may be a 16-byte field for the addresses, a 32-byte field for check sums, and 512 bytes per

1

packet. The semantics of the protocol attach meanings to those fields. For example, if an address field consists of all ones, it is a broadcast packet. Timing, the number of bits per second at which data is sent, is also important, not only at very low levels of protocols, but at high levels of protocols as well.

Figure 1-1 illustrates a diagram of a typical message format. At the beginning of the message, which is flowing one way over the network, some kind of synchronization characters can be assigned so that another node on the network can see that the message is coming and synchronize its receiver with the transmitter. The message header contains addressing information -- where the message is going and where it comes from. The message text itself is information which is going to be sent over the network. It has a header and in some instances a trailer, which is an indication of where the message ends. There may be control and synchronization characters at the end of the message too.

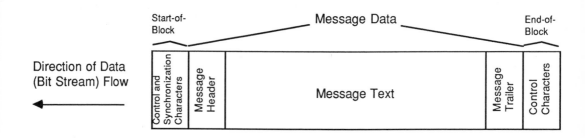

Figure 1-1: Typical Message Format

There are several considerations for end-to-end protocols. One issue is addressing structure: will it be flat so that there is one large addressing space for an interconnected system, or will it be hierarchical so that there is a tree-like structure of addresses such as network, station, and socket within a station? What is the addressing space of the system -- how many nodes, or PCs, can logically be addressed on the system? Despite what many vendors claim, the number of PCs that can be attached to a system is typically far less than the addressing space. What should the data unit size be? There must be a compromise between large and small data unit sizes as large units may "hog" the system and small units may have more overhead. Does the system have some type of error control? If something goes wrong, can the protocol system indicate what the problem is, and does it provide for error recovery? How do packets synchronize themselves in the protocol layers? Suppose someone inadvertently affects someone else's data packet or writes into the wrong file server, is protection provided? Is there protocol monitoring for resource management and performance analysis of the system? As we shall see in later chapters, NETBIOS addresses most, but not all, of these considerations.

1.3 PC Network and Token-Ring Implementations

Applications written to NETBIOS for PC Network will work "as is" with the Token-Ring emulator, but the two networks implement the underlying protocols differently. Example NETBIOS applications available from IBM include the IBM PC Local Area Network Program, the Asynchronous Communications Server, and the SNA 3270 Program. The implementation of NETBIOS for PC Network and the Token-Ring is illustrated in Figure 1-2. The important difference is that NETBIOS in PC Network is totally self-contained on the PC Network Adapter. In the Token-Ring, by contrast, it is contained within the host PC itself. While some debate exists on whether the Token-Ring implementation can perform as well without a dedicated NETBIOS co-processor, preliminary tests by IBM indicate more than a factor of 2 better performance with the Token-Ring NETBIOS emulator.

1.4 The IBM PC LAN Program

The IBM PC Local Area Network Program Version 1.1 (formerly the IBM PC Network Program) is an example "application" that relies on NETBIOS for its operation. It implements the Server Message Block (SMB) protocol. The PC LAN Program provides the user with workstation functions (redirector, receiver, and messenger) and non-dedicated server functions (workstation and server functions). The redirector (which was written by Microsoft and included by IBM in the PC LAN Program) intercepts requests from DOS to determine if the request is for a remote resource. The receiver allows a workstation to receive text messages from other users. The messenger allows one to send messages to other users. The server is a non-dedicated file server which allows a user to share the hard disks and printers associated with his or her PC with others in the network.

1.5 The OSI Reference Model

When talking about NETBIOS and its services, it is useful to refer to the International Standards Organization's reference model for Open Systems Interconnection (OSI). The model is an architecture for the interconnection of computing devices in non- homogeneous environments. It encompasses not only LANS, but other networks as well, such as the wide-area X.25-type networks (e.g., ARPANET, TELENET) and short-haul mainframe networks. A number of

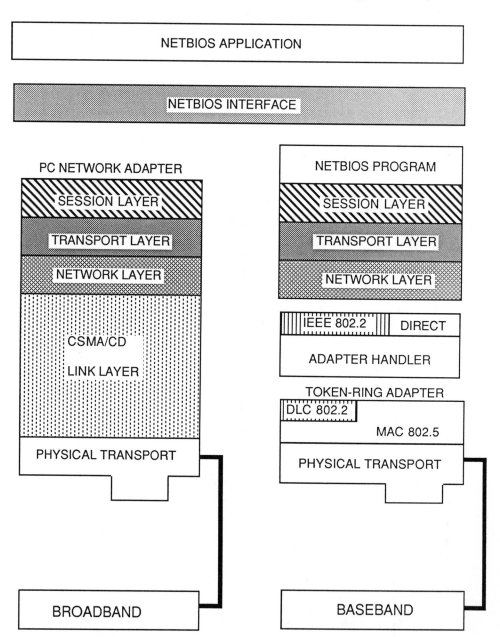

Figure 1-2: NETBIOS Implementation

standards committees, including IEEE and ISO, have constructed the specific syntax and semantics of protocols for the implementation of the various layers.

The OSI model consists of seven layers of protocol as depicted in Figure 1-3. Each layer provides a service to the layer directly above it, and relies on the services of the layer directly below it. (The exception to this rule is, of course, the lowest layer of the model, the physical link). The seven layers are defined briefly below.

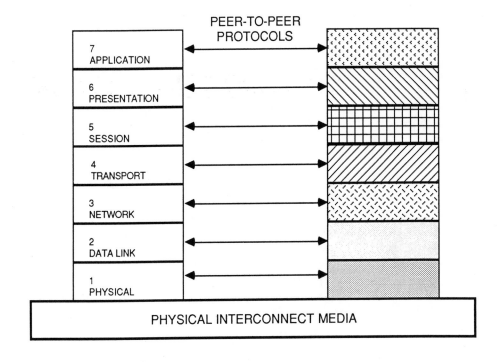

Figure 1-3: The OSI Reference Model

Layer 1 is the physical link layer. It consists of the bit stream of data as sent and received from the network. Included is the raw transmission rate (2.5 Mbps on PC Network, 4 Mbps on Token-Ring) and the encoding scheme (both networks use Manchester encoding, PC Network over a broadband channel, Token-Ring on baseband).

Layer 2 is the data link layer. This layer defines the meaning or structure of the bit stream. The packet format which is described in Layer 2 is actually transmitted over the network using the services of Layer 1. In the Token-Ring, the IEEE 802.2 Logical Link Control (LLC) and IEEE 802.5 Data Link Control (DLC) are used. In PC Network, a proprietary Sytek protocol is used, along with a variation on the IEEE 802.3 DLC (Ethernet).

Layer 3 defines the network layer. The network layer is the lowermost layer of NETBIOS. It is responsible for the routing and switching of data throughout the LAN and interconnected LANs. It must recognize network addresses and be able to route information (packets) to the appropriate networks or pass it up to the transport layer for further interpretation. The session layer is proprietary to Sytek.

Layer 3 is one of the weak spots in NETBIOS. NETBIOS was not designed with internetworking in mind, thus it lacks a number of features needed to support this function efficiently. Internetworking between the PC Network and Token-Ring (as provided by the IBM Interconnect Program) is done by an application that resides in a PC as a gateway, and passes names between systems as well as packets between sessions (in a "store and forward" manner). It is interesting to note that the Interconnect Program can only internet two LANs.

Layer 4 defines the transport layer of the OSI model. It is the middle layer of NETBIOS. The transport layer is responsible for the reliable transfer of information between stations on the network, and it implements features such as acknowledgments, sequence numbers, and time-outs. Again, NETBIOS uses protocols proprietary to Sytek for the implementation of the transport protocols.

Layer 5 is the session layer, the topmost layer of NETBIOS. The interface between NETBIOS and the host PC occurs at this level. The session layer supports naming and establishes sessions or logical links between two names on the network, or even two names within the PC. Like the network and transport layers, the session layer in NETBIOS is a proprietary implementation. The interface to NETBIOS is public domain information, however, and many vendors, including Novell and AST Research, offer NETBIOS emulators for their networks. As long as the interface to the host remains identical, any protocols can be used for the actual peer-to-peer protocols within the layers.

Layer 6 is the presentation layer of the OSI model. It is not part of NETBIOS. The presentation layer is responsible for the negotiation of syntax to be used when passing information to and from the application layer (Layer 7). Included are character formats such as EBCDIC vs. ASCII, and other formats for number representation or file formats. It may have to perform conversion if the application layer format is not compatible with the application layer format of another PC or service on the network.

The presentation layer in a PC Network or Token-Ring with NETBIOS emulation is essentially non-existent. To some extent, PC-DOS is part of the presentation layer since it is the format that is used to communicate with applications. PC-DOS cannot, however, recognize the format of any other files or characters besides its own.

Layer 7 is the application layer. It is responsible for presenting services to the end user. Example applications are the IBM PC Local Area Network Program and the IBM PC Interconnect Program, as discussed briefly above. The IBM PC LAN program relies on PC-DOS 3.2 and NETBIOS for its operation and provides network file and print services to the end user.

OSI Layer Communication

In the OSI model, each layer communicates by passing its data to the layer beneath it; the message header is appended, and then the data packet is passed to the next layer. This process continues until the physical layer is reached; at that point, the entire encapsulated packet is sent out through the network in the form of a bit stream. When the bit stream reaches the receiving node, it becomes de-encapsulated at the data link level. If the data link level recognizes the data packet, and if the address is correct, it will pass the packet up to the next level. This process continues until the data packet reaches the application level. Although it is possible to send thousands of bytes of data at a time through the physical and data link levels, the actual usable data that is sent is far less due to encapsulation and appending of headers in the process.

OSI Layer Interaction

In Figure 1-4, layer "N" interacts with layers "N - 1" and "N + 1" through primitives or parameters that pass back and forth between the layers. Each layer provides a service for the layer above it. Protocols emphasize peer-to-peer level communication within a layer of a protocol: one layer entity communicates with another layer entity.

A level of protocol passes a packet to the level beneath it until it goes through the network and the receiving node. Layer "N" only knows what is happening in layers "N - 1" and "N + 1." It does not what is happening in the other levels of protocol. This means that system implementors can easily change levels of protocol to adapt

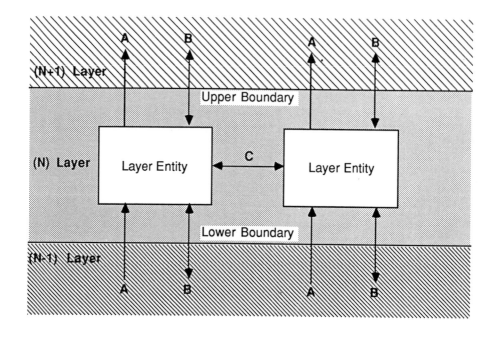

A = Layer Services
B = Primitives/Parameters
C = Peer Protocol

Figure 1-4: OSI Layer Interaction

to new standards and new protocols as they evolve with a minimum impact on the system.

1.6 NETBIOS or APPC/PC?

Like most higher level protocols, NETBIOS is hardware-independent, which means it can be used across a variety of systems. The future of NETBIOS is uncertain, however, in light of IBM's introduction of IBM Advanced Program-to-Program Communication/PC (APPC/PC) for its Token-Ring, which has a much broader appeal over the entire line of IBM computers and communications equipment. APPC (an implementation of Logical Unit 6.2) is of great importance to developers of applications for IBM computers, since IBM offers it for every major computer line it sells and is actively promoting it as an "open" interface.

NETBIOS does have the advantage of having been established in hundreds of PC LANs, while APPC/PC will be catching up in the 1987 to 1988 time frame. Another edge NETBIOS has over APPC is that APPC implements SNA protocols which consume more system resources. One wants to minimize this overhead in a personal computer.

NETBIOS is based on the protocols of Sytek's LocalNet 20, a broadband terminal-to-host LAN. It provides an interface to various levels of International Standards Organization (ISO) protocol to the host. Most NETBIOS services are provided at the session level. Session services supported include peer-to-peer communication and naming. Additional services are supported at three lower levels -- network, transport, and link.

1.7 Relationship to PC-DOS and Applications

In order to allow applications to share information in a NETBIOS- based LAN, three important pieces of systems software are included: 1) PC-DOS 3.1 or greater for the PC Network, 3.2 or greater for the Token-Ring; 2) NETBIOS itself; and 3) the redirector. The manner in which PC-DOS, NETBIOS, and redirector fit into a system is illustrated in Figure 1-5. NET, accessible from an application or the redirector via interrupt 2AH, is part of the IBM PC Local Area Network Program. A complete implementation of the PC Network Program is given on the right side of the figure; the file and print server is shown executing as an application in the background.

An application can actually do one of three operations as far as the network is concerned: a user application (such as a word processor) will call DOS and have the redirector send I/O to/from a server via the NET program; a "multi-user" word processor will use the extended DOS calls to lock/unlock files; a specialized server application will call NETBIOS directly using the interrupt 5CH. A fourth option is for an application to directly call the file/print server, if it is implemented, using the interrupts 2AH or 2FH.

A summary of the functions provided by interrupts 2FH, 21H, and 2AH are given in Figure 1-6. The 5CH NETBIOS interrupt will be discussed in greater detail in later chapters.

1.8 NETBIOS Protocols

It is stressed that the NETBIOS option available for the Token-Ring is an emulation of the NETBIOS contained within the PC Network Adapter card. Therefore, while the actual protocols used within the various layers may differ between the Token-

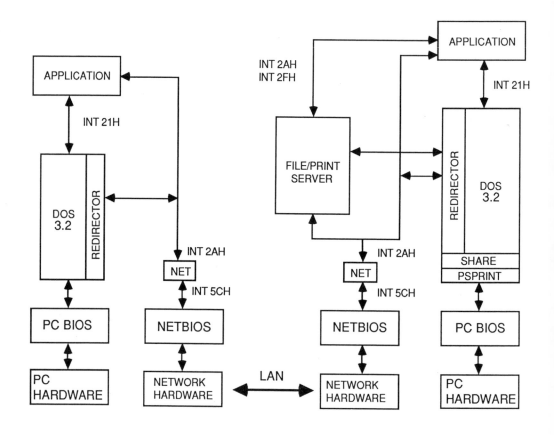

Figure 1-5: NETBIOS/DOS Service

Ring and the PC Network, what the user or programmer sees is identical interfaces and operation, with the exception that the response time is much faster in the Token-Ring.

On the Token-Ring, the host processor must operate the protocols, whereas on the IBM PC Network, an on-board 80188 processor does the protocol processing. Interestingly, NETBIOS tests on both networks have shown the Token-Ring implementation to operate more than a factor of two better than PC Network in terms of raw data rate. This is largely due to overhead between the four micro-processors on the PC Network Adapter, and the way in which the NETBIOS protocols were programmed.

AX Register

□ AH ▨ AL

All Values Shown in HEX

Interrupt 2F

	00	NET Command Installation Check
BB	03	Get Server Post Address
	04	Set Server Post Address

Interrupt 2A

00	Installation Check .
01	Execute NETBIOS Request
02	Set NET Printer Mode
03	Get Device Shared Status

Interrupt 21

3D		Open File with Sharing Specified
	09	Is Device Redirected?
44	0A	Is Handle Local or Remote?
	0B	Change Sharing Retry Count
59		Get Extended Error
5A		Create Temp File with Unique Name
5B		Create New File
5C	00	Lock Byte Range
	01	Unlock Byte Range
5E	00	Get Machine Name
	02	Set Up Printer Control String
	02	Get Assign List Entry
5F	03	Redirect Device to NET
	04	Cancel Redirection

Figure 1-6: Summary of Interrupt Functions 2FH, 21H, and 2AH

The host PC communicates with NETBIOS via the Network Control Block (NCB). (The format and operation of the NCB is detailed in Chapter 2.) Once the NCB is set up by the host, it interrupts NETBIOS for service. NETBIOS then takes over and invokes the necessary protocols to perform the service requested by the host (although some services -- such as a request to perform local diagnostics or to obtain the adapter's address -- may not require protocols).

NETBIOS uses four levels of protocol -- data link, network, transport, and session -- Layers 2 through 5 with respect to the OSI Reference Model. The way Sytek implemented NETBIOS, the host appears to be communicating with only the session layer, but in reality, many of the requests are simply passed to the lower layers.

The data link layer provides the link access protocol (LAP) to PC Network or Token-Ring. This is where a major discrepancy exists between the two networks in terms of NETBIOS implementation. The Token-Ring provides the IEEE standard 802.2 Data Link Control (DLC) and 802.5 Media Access Control (MAC). The PC Network provides a proprietary DLC and 802.3 Media Access Control (CSMA/CD and frame format). LAP is used to provide service for the packet transfer protocol (PTP).

The PTP implements the network layer. PTP provides routing, address discovery, and unacknowledged packet transfer services (datagrams). PTP is used by the reliable stream protocol (RSP) and the datagram transport protocol (DTP).

PTP is a weakness of the PC Network in that the "routing" function is a simplistic name-mapping scheme, and it has not been altered or improved in order to preserve complete NETBIOS compatibility on the Token-Ring. PTP does not have the facilities to implement internetworking, making gateways between two networks difficult to implement and limited in functionality. For example, the PC Network to Token-Ring Interconnect Program can link only two networks together with a maximum of just 16 "services" between them.

RSP resides at the transport layer. It provides error-free virtual connection services to other users through end-to-end acknowledgments and retransmissions. RSP provides transport layer services to the session management protocol (SMP). Datagram transport protocol (DTP) also resides at this level. It provides unacknowledged datagram services between session layer entities, including the user datagram protocol (UDP) and the diagnostic and monitoring protocol (DMP).

The session layer provides host access to several protocols. The session management protocol (SMP) provides support for user sessions between nodes. SMP allows users to establish connection to a named process. It is responsible for interacting with the name management protocol (NMP) within the local node to determine the address of the named process. Once the destination node is determined, the initiating SMP can communicate with the SMP within the destination node to provide session level services.

In conjunction with naming, the user datagram protocol (UDP) provides support for datagrams between two names (nodes). The name management protocol (NMP) provides the binding of alias names and network addresses within the entire local network. NMP provides all name management services, including the translation of remote names to network addresses. This part of the protocol is one reason why it takes so long to become part of a NETBIOS network when starting up -- the node will broadcast its names to the other stations a number of times to make sure all other stations on the name "receive" it. This also occurs when SMP has to establish a connection with another name.

One of the more interesting protocols provided by the session layer is the diagnostic and monitoring protocol (DMP). DMP allows the collection of diagnostic and status information. DMP can actually query other adapter cards via the network to find out their state.

The general operation of the protocols and packet formats used by NETBIOS is detailed in Chapter 3. All of these protocols are emulated by the Token-Ring NETBIOS emulator and are proprietary. Vendors such as AST Research and Novell have developed NETBIOS emulators for non-IBM hardware using XNS as the underlying protocols. If the Token-Ring obsoletes PC Network, then IBM is likely to make its Token-Ring NETBIOS emulator open by providing source code, just as the company does now for the IBM PC and IBM PC AT BIOS.

Chapter 2 - Programming

The general procedure
Interfacing with Network Command Block (NCB)
Detailed descriptions of all NETBIOS commands
A list of possible NETBIOS error codes
Implementation differences between PC Network and Token-Ring

2.1 The General Procedure

End-user applications that reside above Layer 7 of the OSI model require no knowledge of NETBIOS. Custom network applications that reside at Layer 7 (such as the DOS-provided file and record locking) require more functionality than provided by PC-DOS; they require detailed knowledge of what NETBIOS does, how it behaves, and how to interface to it. These applications typically require direct sending and receiving of messages between stations. A prime example of a custom network application would be a server that services communications (such as RS-232 ports or a 3274 controller on a PC) or provides access to peripherals such as large-capacity removable hard disks.

To use NETBIOS directly, a station name should be added to the name table. A station name is a unique name by which a given station is known on the network. Alternatively, one can simply use the permanent node address (a unique 48-bit address in ROM assigned to that adapter), in which case a "name" does not have to be entered. Assigning a phonetic name will make a station's name more meaningful, however. On PC Network, each adapter can hold up to 16 names. On the Token-Ring, at least 32 names can be held.

After the station's name is set, a session may be established with another name on the network. The name could already exist in the name table of the station, in which case a "local" session is established. Usually, however, sessions will be established with "remote" names, such as a server session on another machine.

Once the session is established, messages can be sent and received over that logical link. Reliable data transfer is provided in which all messages are acknowledged; otherwise, one can opt for datagram transfer, which means NETBIOS will send the message directly to the data link layer and not be concerned with acknowledgments. Datagram service is useful for broadcasting messages.

2.2 The Programming Interface

This section discusses the programming interface from an applications viewpoint. In the PC Network, NETBIOS is in ROM on the adapter card.

In the Token-Ring, NETBIOS is loaded at the PC-DOS command prompt, using the COM file NETBEUI (NETBIOS Extended User Interface). The format for NETBEUI is: NETBEUI work0, SAP0, stn0, work1, SAP1, stn1. The parameters have the following meaning:

work0/work1:

The amount of PC work storage (RAM) assigned to an adapter, from 1Kb to 18Kb. 18Kb is recommended for a PC that will also function as a server. Since two adapters are supported, work0 and work1 are work areas for the respective adapters. A restriction is that work0 plus work1 must be less than 18Kb. If this parameter is not supplied, 9Kb is used by default.

SAP0/SAP1:

Service access point (a reference point for connection between two nodes at the logical link -- or Layer 2 -- level for adapter 0/adapter 1. These are the additional SAPs requested on an implicit OPEN. Up to 9 additional SAPs may be requested to support non-NETBIOS applications. The default is 0.

stn0/stn1:

The number of additional link stations (up to 9) requested on an implicit OPEN. It equates stns to the number of additional non- NETBIOS remote SAPs that other applications might expect to communicate with at any one time.

NETBEUI occupies approximately 46Kb of RAM in the host PC's memory.

An application requiring NETBIOS services will set up a Network Control Block (NCB) (referred to as the Message Control Block (MCB) in the Token-Ring) and issue a 5CH interrupt. The structure of the NCB and the general meaning of each field is illustrated in Figure 2-1. If the adapter has not been previously initialized by loading the Token-Ring Adapter Support Interface called TOKREUI (Token-Ring Extended User Interface), NETBIOS will do so automatically. The interpretation and operation of each field is detailed as follows.

NCB_COMMAND

When an application issues commands to NETBIOS, it may choose to wait for them

Field Name	Length (in bytes) and Meaning	
NCB_COMMAND	1	- NCB COMMAND FIELD
NCB_RETCODE	1	- NCB RETURN CODE FIELD
NCB_LSN	1	- NCB LOCAL SESSION NUMBER FIELD
NCB_NUM	1	- NCB NUMBER OF YOUR NAME
NCB_BUFFER@	4	- NCB POINTER TO MESSAGE BUFFER ADDRESS (OFFSET:SEGMENT)
NCB_LENGTH	2	- NCB BUFFER LENGTH (IN BYTES)
NCB_CALLNAME	16	- NCB NAME ON LOCAL OR REMOTE ADAPTER - FOR CHAIN SEND THE FIRST 2 BYTES INDICATES LENGTH OF SECOND BUFFER THE NEXT 4 BYTES INDICATES THE BUFFER ADDRESS SECOND
NCB_NAME	16	- NCB NAME ON LOCAL ADAPTER
NCB_RTO	1	- NCB RECEIVE TIMEOUT VALUE
NCB_STO	1	- NCB SEND TIMEOUT VALUE
NCB_POST@	4	- NCB POINTER TO POST ROUTINE (OFFSET:SEGMENT)
NCB_LANA_NUM	1	- NCB ADAPTER NUMBER; 00H FOR FIRST ADAPTER, 01H FOR SECOND ADAPTER
NCB_CMD_ CPLT	1	- NCB COMMAND STATUS FIELD
NCB_ RESERVE	14	- NCB RESERVED AREA

Figure 2-1: Network Control Block (NCB)

to be completed or be interrupted upon completion. This is determined by setting the high-order bit of the command to 1 for no-wait, or 0 for wait. With the wait operation, control is not returned to the next instruction until NETBIOS completes the command. The AL register or NCB_RETCODE field must then be checked for the status of the completed command. The preferable approach is the no-wait option, since NETBIOS essentially executes as a background task, and multiple commands can be queued up. Control is returned the next instruction of the application, with a return code in AL.

The possible return codes are: 00H - successful command completion; 03H-command invalid; 21H - interface is busy; 22H - too many commands queued; 23H - invalid NCB_LANA_NUM field; 24H - command completed while a cancel is occurring; 26H - command cannot be cancelled; 4XH - "unusual network condition"; 50-FEH - adapter has malfunctioned. Return code values of 40H - 4FH are unique to the Token-Ring implementation of NETBIOS and are described with the various commands listed below.

The application can choose to be interrupted upon a 00H (OK) return code, or "poll" the NCB_CMD_CPLT field (initially set to FFH while the command is executing). If the interrupt option is chosen, then the NCB_POST@ field must be set (non-zero). If interrupted, the application can check AL or NCB_RETCODE for the final return code from NETBIOS.

NCB_RETCODE

The return code is mirrored from the code returned in the AL register. See above for possible return code values. If the return code is not 00H, then the application should take appropriate error recovery action.

NCB_LSN

After performing a CALL or LISTEN command, this field indicates the assigned local session number. This field must be set when issuing a SEND or RECEIVE command for that session. NETBIOS assigns the number sequentially, wrapping at 254 back to 1 (255 or FFH and 0 are never used).

NCB_NUM

The number associated with a name. It is returned after requesting an ADD NAME or ADD GROUP NAME. As with NCB_LSN, NETBIOS assigns the number sequentially, wrapping at 254 back to 1. This number must be used when sending datagrams and for RECEIVE ANY.

NCB_BUFFER@

If required by the command (such as SEND), NCB_BUFFER@ is a 4- byte pointer that denotes the offset:segment address of the buffer to be used with that command.

NCB_LENGTH

Length, in bytes of the buffer (pointed to by NCB_BUFFER). For the SEND commands, it is the length of the actual number of bytes to be sent. For receive commands, NETBIOS sets it to the actual number of bytes received.

18

NCB_CALLNAME

The 16-byte name of the session with which one is communicating. When doing a chain send, the first 2 bytes specify the length, and the next 4 bytes specify the buffer address, in the same format as NCB_BUFFER@.

NCB_NAME

The station user's 16-byte name. If the permanent node address is used, then the first 10 bytes are set to 0, followed by the 48-bit (6 byte) node address.

NCB_RTO

Specifies the receive time-out in 500 ms increments before a RECEIVE command times-out. A value of 0 is no time-out. NCB_RTO is fixed once a session is established.

NCB_STO

Like NCB_RTO, except for SEND commands.

NCB_POST@

The offset:segment address of the routine to be executed after NETBIOS has completed a no-wait command. The application must set up the POST routine, and the POST routine, the DS register. The standard interrupt return instruction, IRET, is used upon completion of the POST routine. If NCB_POST@ is 0, then NETBIOS does not invoke the POST routine, and the application has to monitor the NCB_CMD_CPLT field.

NCB_LANA_NUM

Used to indicated which adapter the command is for. A 00H is used for the first, and a 01H is used for the second.

NCB_CMD_CPLT

A value of FFH indicates that the command has not yet be executed. A value of 00H indicates completion. As noted above, a non-zero value indicates an error.

NCB_RESERVE

A 14-byte reserved space, used partially by the Token-Ring implementation of NETBIOS.

2.3 NETBIOS Commands

The commands which can be executed by NETBIOS can be broken up into four groups: general, name support, session support, and datagram support. General commands are non-communicating commands that deal primarily with the adapter itself. Name support commands allow applications to associate resources and services with logical names instead of discrete addresses. Session commands allow an application to establish a reliable link between two names for communicating information. Again, keep in mind that a session link may be within an adapter or with a name on a remote adapter. Datagram commands allow the broadcasting of short (less than 512 byte) messages as well as the sending of unacknowledged messages to another name.

A summary of the possible commands follows. Note that in addition to the fields required by each command as outlined here, the NCB_COMMAND field must be set to the appropriate number as indicated (in hex notation) the adapter number (0 or 1) must be selected by setting NCB_LANA_NUM, and all of the NETBIOS commands must return a result in the NCB_RETCODE field.

Command   NCB_COMMAND   Function

General Commands

RESET   32H   Resets local adapter status and clears name and session tables.

By resetting the adapter, an application can change the number of sessions and the number of NCB command blocks supported by NETBIOS. The default power-on for PC Network values are 6 and 12, respectively. These numbers must be carefully set or else performance may suffer, since more sessions and NCB command blocks could mean smaller packet sizes, depending on how much adapter memory there is.

The only NCB fields (other than NCB_COMMAND and NCB_LANA_NUM) required for RESET are NCB_LSN, NCB_NUM.

CANCEL   35H   Requests that pending command whose NCB can be found at NCB_BUFFER@ be cancelled.

One can cancel any pending NETBIOS command except ADD [GROUP] NAME, DELETE NAME, SEND DATAGRAM, SEND BROADCAST DATAGRAM, SESSION STATUS, CANCEL, AND RESET. Cancelling a SEND command will also drop the session. NCB_BUFFER@ is required (the buffer to be canceled).

20

STATUS   33H (wait)   Gives status information for local or B3H
(return) remote adapter.

STATUS provides status information for local or remote adapters. This command can be used to perform diagnostics on local as well as remote adapters, even if the remote PC cannot communicate properly with its adapter, or is in a "hung" state. Fields required include NCB_BUFFER@, NCB_LENGTH, NCB_CALLNAME, and NCB_POST@ (for no-wait option only).

The information returned in the buffer for PC Network includes the 6-byte permanent node address, the 1-byte status of external jumpers on the network adapter card, the 1-byte results of the last self-test, 2 bytes containing the software revision number, 48 bytes of traffic and error statistics, 26 bytes of adapter resource statistics, 2 bytes for the number of names in the local table, and 16 entries of 18 bytes each for the local name table.

The traffic and error statistics returned for PC Network include 2 bytes for the reporting period (in minutes), 2 bytes for the number of CRC errors, 2 bytes for the number of alignment errors, 2 bytes for the number of collisions, 2 bytes for the number of aborted transmissions, 4 bytes for the number of successfully transmitted packets, 4 bytes for the number of successfully received packets, 2 bytes for the number of retransmissions, and 2 bytes for the number of times the receiver has exhausted its resources.

The adapter resource statistics returned for PC Network include 8 bytes of reserved space, 2 bytes for the number of free command blocks, 2 bytes for the maximum configured NCBs, 2 bytes for the maximum free command blocks, 4 bytes reserved, 2 bytes for the number of pending sessions, 2 bytes for the maximum pending sessions, 2 bytes for the total maximum number of sessions, and 2 bytes for the maximum session data packet size.

TRACE   79H (wait)   Token-Ring only.
           F9H (return)

TRACE activates a trace of all MCB commands and some of the control block (CCB) commands issued by the NETBIOS program.

UNLINK   70H   Used with remote program load (RPL) to
unlink session with IBMNETBOOT.

UNLINK is used only if a call to IBMNETBOOT was made when the PC was powered on, i.e., a remote boot was performed. The session with IBMNETBOOT is dropped and the redirector (INT 13) is dropped.

Name Support Commands

Names allow an application and the PC upon which it runs to be known by other applications and PCs on the network. Names are 16 bytes long and can be entered into the local name table; up to 16 names are allowed on PC Network and at least 32 on Token-Ring. A name that is unique to a PC can also be part of a group (a group name). Recall that each station is always assigned a permanent node name (6 bytes of address followed by 10 zeros) by default. An application can retrieve this name by performing an ADAPTER STATUS command with an asterisk in the callname field. The first 6 bytes in the return buffer indicate the address of the adapter. Both PC Network and Token-Ring use 6-byte node addresses.

ADD NAME 30H (wait)   Adds a (unique) 16-character name to B0H
                                 (return) name table.

A broadcast is performed by NETBIOS to ensure that the name is unique. The NCB field NCB_POST@ is required if the no-wait option is used. Error codes are returned to indicate a full table, duplicate name, a name that is not unique, etc.

ADD GROUP 36H (wait)   Adds a group name to the name table.
 NAME   B6H (return)

A broadcast is performed by NETBIOS to ensure than the name is not being used as a unique name on another PC. NCB fields and error conditions are the same as ADD NAME.

Since names can be up to 16 bytes in length, and the actual address size (at the data link layer) is only 6 bytes, NETBIOS will derive a group address for itself using one of two methods.

The first method requires applying the following function:

group_name = 0000 concat (N1 xor N2 ... N5 xor N6) concat FF

where N1 ... N5 are the first through first five char fields of the name and N6 is the last char of the name.

The second method is to derive the group address from the permanent node name by applying the following function:

group_name = 0000 concat (ID3 ID2 ID1) concat FF

where ID3 ... ID1 are the three low-order bytes of the permanent node name.

These addresses derived by NETBIOS are not normally available to the application, but can be calculated using the above formulas. The above formulas were chosen to minimize the chance that two different 16-byte names will "hash" down to the same 6-byte group address.

DELETE	31H (wait)	Deletes name from name table.
NAME	B1H (return)	

DELETE removes a name that was entered by ADD NAME or ADD GROUP NAME from the local name table. DELETE NAME is typically performed after terminating a session with the HANG UP command (described below). If there are still active sessions, NETBIOS will delay the delete until all active sessions are terminated. NCB_POST@ is required if the no-wait option is used.

Session Support Commands

The session commands form the heart of NETBIOS and are responsible for the actual passing of information (up to 65,535 bytes per request) over the network. Sessions commands are used to establish a link between any two names on the network, or even within the PC itself. Up to 32 sessions on PC Network and at least 32 sessions on Token-Ring can be active simultaneously. Note that names are used to initiate the process, but NETBIOS returns a number in the NCB_LSN field that is used from then on.

CALL	10H (wait)	Opens a session with another name
	90H (return)	specified by the NCB_CALLNAME field.

CALL initiates a session with the name specified in the NCB_CALLNAME field, using the local name supplied by the NCB_NAME field. When CALLing another name, it must have already set up a LISTEN command. NETBIOS returns a session number in the NCB_LSN field. NCB fields required include NCB_RTO (receive time-out), NCB_STO (send time-out), and NCB_POST@ if the no-wait option is used.

23

LISTEN	11H (wait)	Enables a session to be established
	91H (return)	with the name specified in the
		NCB_CALLNAME field.

The complement of CALL, LISTEN allows a session to be established with the name in the NCB_CALLNAME field and the name in the NCB_NAME field. NCB_CALLNAME can be set to an asterisk, in which case any name is accepted from a CALL. The name that initiated the CALL is then returned in the NCB_CALLNAME field. It is important to note that a LISTEN occupies a session entry. Fields required include NCB_NAME, NCB_RTO (receive time-out), NCB_STO (send time-out), and NCB_POST@ if the no-wait option is used.

| HANG UP | 12H (wait) | Closes the session with another name. |
| | 92H (return) | |

HANG UP terminates a session and all pending RECEIVE commands. NCB_POST@ is required for the no-wait option.

| SEND | 14H (wait) | Sends data by the session number |
| | 94H (return) | indicated in the local session number (LSN). |

This command sends (reliably) up to a 65,535 byte buffer pointed to by NCB_BUFFER@ via the session indicated by NCB_LSN. Multiple SEND commands can be queued. If the SEND cannot complete, the session is terminated and must be re-established.

CHAIN	17H (wait)	Like SEND, except that data is taken SEND
	97H (return)	from the buffers for the indicated number of
		bytes. Two buffers can be chained together.

NETBIOS actually sends the buffers as one concatenated message and the size limit is still 65,535 bytes. NCB_CALLNAME is used to specify the length (first 2 bytes) and address (next 4 bytes) of the second buffer. Fields required include NCB_BUFFER@, NCB_LENGTH, NCB_CALLNAME (0000H length format, 00000000H address format), and NCB_POST@ if the no-wait option is used.

| RECEIVE | 15H (wait) | Receive data from a specified session. |
| | 95H (return) | Time-out values can be specified. |

RECEIVE sets up the adapter for receiving data from a specific session. If the

24

received data exceeds the available buffer size, then a code of 06H is returned in the NCB_RETCODE field. Fields required include NCB_BUFFER@, NCB_LENGTH, and NCB_POST@ if the no- wait option is used.

RECEIVE	16H (wait)	Receive data from any station with which ANY
	96H (return)	a session has been established.

Like RECEIVE, except that it allows data to be received from any session. NCB_NUM (as returned from ADD NAME or ADD GROUP NAME) must be used instead of a name. Fields required are the same as RECEIVE.

SESSION	34H (wait)	Obtain status of all active sessions STATUS
	B4H (return)	for station name.

SESSION STATUS returns status information on all active sessions for a given local name (NCB_NAME) or all local names (if an asterisk is placed in the first byte of the NCB_NAME field). Fields required include NCB_BUFFER@, NCB_LENGTH, AND NCB_POST@ if the no-wait option is used.

The format of the returned status information is as follows: 1 byte for the number of sessions being reported; 1 byte for the number of sessions with this name; 1 byte for the number of datagram commands pending; 1 byte for the number of RECEIVE ANY commands pending; 36 bytes for the information about a session, including 1 byte for the local session number, 1 byte for the state of the session (01H = LISTEN pending; 02H = CALL pending; 03H = session establish; 04H = HANG UP pending; 05H = HANG UP complete; 06H = session aborted); 16 bytes for the local name; 16 bytes for the remote name; 1 byte for the number of RECEIVE commands pending; and 1 byte for the number of SEND and CHAIN SEND commands pending.

Datagram Support Commands

The last group of NETBIOS commands is for datagrams. Datagrams allow the user to send unacknowledged messages of up to 512 bytes to a name or group name, or broadcast to all names.

SEND	20H (wait)	Send a datagram to a unique name or
DATAGRAM	A0H (return)	group name at a local or remote node.

SEND DATAGRAM sends a datagram to a name or group name. That name must be set up for a RECEIVE DATAGRAM. Fields required include NCB_BUFFER@, NCB_LENGTH, NCB_NUM, and the optional NCB_POST@ for the no-wait.

SEND	22H (wait)	Send a message to everyone who has a
BROADCAST	A2H (return)	RECEIVE BROADCAST DATAGRAM
		outstanding. DATAGRAM

SEND BROADCAST DATAGRAM sends a broadcast message that is picked up by any application that has a RECEIVE BROADCAST DATAGRAM pending. Fields required are the same as SEND DATAGRAM.

RECEIVE	21H (wait)	Receive a datagram message from any
DATAGRAM	A1H (return)	name or anyone on the network.

RECEIVE DATAGRAM receives any datagram addressed to a local name or group name at that PC. The fields required are the same as SEND DATAGRAM. If NCB_NUM is set to FFH, then a datagram can be received from any name for any of the local names.

RECEIVE	23H (wait)	Receive a datagram from anyone who
BROADCAST	A3H (return)	issues a SEND BROADCAST DATAGRAM
DATAGRAM		command.

RECEIVE BROADCAST DATAGRAM receives any BROADCAST DATAGRAM. Fields required are the same as SEND DATAGRAM.

2.4 NETBIOS Error Codes

Figure 2-2 is a listing of the possible error codes returned by NETBIOS when the application uses the NCB and interrupt 5CH.

NETBIOS on PC Network does not implement the standard 802.2 DLC or MAC. Therefore on the Token-Ring, NETBIOS has been assigned an architected functional address of 00000080H to satisfy 802.2 requirements. With the NETBIOS program operational, all adapters with a functional address set will receive all frames destined for that address. The architected service access point (SAP) value is F0H. Frames destined for Data Link Control (DLC) SAP F0H will be routed to the NETBIOS program whether received through functional address or specific node address detection.

Value (in Hex)	Meaning
00H	Good return; command complete.
01H	Invalid buffer length for SEND DATAGRAM, SEND BROADCAST, ADAPTER STATUS, OR SESSION STATUS.
03H	Illegal command code.
05H	Command time-out period has expired.
06H	Message received was partial since receive buffer was not large enough.
08H	Session number specified is not active.
09H	Not enough space available in adapter for session.
0AH	Session is closed.
0BH	Command was cancelled.
0DH	Duplicate name in local name table.
0EH	Local name table is full.
0FH	Name to be deleted is active in a session.
11H	Local session table is full.
12H	Session open was rejected since no LISTEN is outstanding on remote computer.
13H	Illegal name number.
14H	Cannot find name called or there is no answer.
15H	Name not found in local table.
16H	Name is in use elsewhere.
17H	Name deleted with no outstanding commands for that name.
18H	Session ended abnormally.
19H	NETBIOS has detected two or more identical names in use on network!
1AH	Incompatible packet protocol received.
21H	Interface is busy.
22H	Too many commands are outstanding.
23H	Bad number in NCB_LANA_NUM field.
24H	Command completed before cancel request or command never existed.
26H	Command is illegal to cancel.
4XH	Undeterminable network error.
50-FEH	Adapter has malfunctioned.
FFH	Command is still pending.

Figure 2-2: NETBIOS Error Return Codes

Since NETBIOS on the Token-Ring is not implemented in firmware in the adapter as it is for PC Network, it poses a number of special considerations. Initializing the adapter handler can be done explicitly by an application in which an established shared RAM address is used and the error appendages (interrupt handlers) are defined by the application, or implicitly by the NETBIOS program when a RESET is encountered or the first MCB is encountered. In this case, shared RAM addresses D8000H/D4000H for adapters 00/01 will be used, and NETBIOS will define error appendages.

OPEN CCB is an optional NETBIOS call that is used to define a set of NETBIOS program specific parameters. OPEN CCB can be done explicitly by an application. It must be issued before the first NCB and after NETBIOS is loaded. OPEN CCB can be done explicitly by a RESET or first NCB.

A typical Token-Ring initialize sequence would be as follows: NETBIOS (NETBEUI) issues (to TOKREUI) DIR.INITIALIZE, issues DIR.OPEN. ADAPTER, issues DIR.STATUS, issues DLC.OPEN.SAP (with SAP set to F0H), issues DIR.SET.FUNCTIONAL.ADDRESS, issues DLC.MODIFY, and issues SET.TIMER.

The following is the sequence of NETBIOS events that occurs when an application issues a NETBIOS command (via the NCB) to establish a session: NETBEUI issues (to TOKREUI) DIR.SET.TIMER (for name recognized response), issues DIR.TRANSMIT.UI (broadcast NAME.QUERY), returns immediate return code if no-wait NCB, RECEIVE data response (name recognized), issues DIR. CANCEL.TIMER, issues DIR.FREE.BUFFER, issues DLC.OPEN.STATION (establishes link station), issues DLC.CONNECT_STATION (connects the nodes), issues DIR.TRANSMIT.FRAME (sends session initialize), RECEIVE data response (session confirmed), returns final NCB return code.

There are a number of subtle differences in the PC Network NETBIOS and the Token-Ring NETBIOS emulation. The Token-Ring implementation contains a few enhancements that should not be used if one wishes to maintain compatibility with the PC Network. These differences are listed here.

Token-Ring NETBIOS	PC Network NETBIOS
TRACE command for diagnostics	--
FIND command to locate any 16-character name on the network	--
UNLINK does not apply to Token-	UNLINK for RPL

Ring adapter boards that do
not support Remote Program
Load (RPL)

32 links per adapter	16 links per adapter
254 sessions per adapter	32 sessions per adapter
254 names	16 names
255 outstanding MCBs	32 outstanding NCBs

The Token-Ring NETBIOS emulator also has a number of additional NETBIOS Return Codes. When the following return codes are set in the MCB, the emulator will also return related status in the MCB RESERVE field.

Extended Return Code	Meaning
4EH	Ring status not temporary
4FH	Permanent ring status error
F7H	Error on implicit INITIALIZE
F8H	Error on implicit OPEN
F9H	TOKREUI internal error
FAH	Adapter machine check
FBH	NETBEUI code not present
FCH	OPEN adapter or OPEN_SAP failed
FDH	Unexpected CLOSE of adapter

Both a PC Network adapter and Token-Ring adapter may coexist in the same PC. If a PC Network adapter is present and operational, all NCB commands issued for that adapter number will be routed to it. If a PC Network adapter is not present, then all NCB commands issued for that adapter number will be routed to the Token-Ring

NETBIOS program if installed. If neither are present, the adapter handler (TOKREUI) will return an FBH in the NCB.

On both PC Network and Token-Ring, the user can jumper select which adapter is the primary (00) adapter and which adapter is the secondary (01) adapter.

Chapter 3 - Protocols

Protocols and packet formats used by the PC Network NETBIOS
The session layer
The transport layer
The network layer

3.1 Protocols and Packet Formats

The groundwork for the basic operation of the NETBIOS protocols was given in Chapter One. Figure 3-1 illustrates the dependencies between the various protocols.

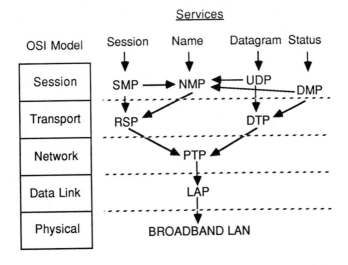

Legend:
SMP: Session Management Protocol
UDP: User Datagram Protocol
NMP: Name Management Protocol
DMP: Diagnostic and Monitoring Protocol
RSP: Reliable Stream Protocol
DTP: Datagram Transport Protocol
PTP: Packet Transfer Protocol
LAP: Link Access Protocol

Figure 3-1: Protocol Relationships

31

The basic operation for exchanging information between two names on the network is as follows. First, the names must be added to the respective application's local name table at that PC. Then a session must be established between the two names using the CALL and LISTEN commands. Data transfer can then occur using the SEND and RECEIVE commands. Lastly, the session is terminated using the HANG UP or RESET commands. A generic timing of packet exchanges is illustrated in Figure 3-2.

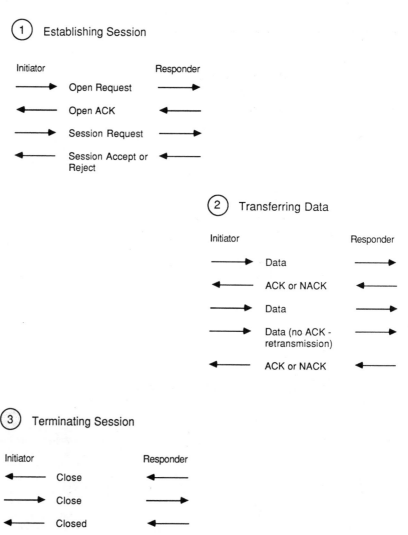

Figure 3-2: Generic Packet Timing

3.2 Session Layer NETBIOS Commands/Protocol Actions

In the following section, the actions taken by NETBIOS for various NCB commands will be examined. The commands and protocols are associated with the IBM PC Network Session Management Protocol (SMP). What essentially is given here is a high-level description of the protocols used by SMP. The packet formats are also given when they are first referenced. The formats are the ones used by the IBM PC Network NETBIOS; they may be different for other implementations.

All packets received by NETBIOS have already gone through CRC checking and address recognition at the data link level. In the case of the IBM PC Network, this is done by the Intel 82586 CSMA controller. With the Token-Ring, it is done by proprietary IBM protocol handlers.

ADD NAME

NETBIOS checks the name to make sure it is valid and continues if it is okay. If it doesn't find the name in the local name table, it broadcasts a "name claim" packet (Figure 3-3) several times to ensure that all stations see the request. If a response is received, the packet is in the form of Figure 3-4. If a response is not received, NETBIOS adds the name to the local name table.

START DEL 7EH	DEST ADDR 6	SOURCE ADDR 6	LENGTH 2	Value of 5000H	Claim=10H Cancel=A0H	# of packets willing to accept 0?H	CONNECTION ID 2	• • •

Value of 0202H	Don't Care 2	Value of 0400H	Don't Care 4	Value of 10XXH	Value of 0000H	ASCII DEST NAME 16	PREV NET CONN ID 2	• • •

RETRANSMIT COUNT 2	SOURCE NODE CONNECTION ID 2	DEST ID 6	SOURCE ID 6	PREV NODE ID 6	• • •

CRC 4	END-OF-FRAME Value of 7EH

Figure 3-3: Name Claim/Name Cancel Packet

START DEL 7EH	DEST ADDR 6	SOURCE ADDR 6	LENGTH 2	Value of 4000H	Value of 30H	# of packets willing to accept 0?H	CONNECTION ID 2	•••

Don't Care 2	Reason why packet NAK 1	Don't Care 1	Value of 0400H	Don't Care 4	Value of 10XXH	Value of 0000H	ASCII DEST NAME 16	•••

DEST NODE CONNECTION ID 2	CRC 4	END-OF-FRAME Value of 7EH

Figure 3-4: Name Claim Response Packet

DELETE NAME

As with ADD NAME, NETBIOS checks for a valid name and continues if it is okay. If a non-active session is found associated with that name, it is terminated. Otherwise the delete request is queued until the "session count" (active sessions) is zero, in which case the name is then removed from the name table.

CALL

NETBIOS first checks to make sure that the local name is found in the name table. If it is found, NETBIOS checks for the remote name in the name table, and if it is not found, broadcasts a "name query" packet (Figure 3-5) to the network. If the remote name is found or a node responds to the name query broadcasts, then a "session request" packet (Figure 3-6) is sent to the destination and a LISTEN command is executed to wait for the reply. If a "session accept" packet (Figure 3-7) is received before LISTEN times-out, then NETBIOS sets a session_established flag in the session table, returns the local session number (LSN) to the application, and returns the command completed status (CMD_CPLT) to the application.

LISTEN/LISTEN ANY

NETBIOS first checks to make sure that the local name is found in the name table. If it is found, NETBIOS makes sure that room is available in the session table and waits for a "session request" packet. If the source of the "session request" packet is the same as the remote name specified by the application, then LISTEN is completed, a "session accept" packet is returned to the source, the

START DEL 7EH	DEST ADDR 6	SOURCE ADDR 6	LENGTH 2	Value of 5000H	Value of 10H	# of packets willing to accept 0?H	CONNECTION ID 2	...

Value of 0202H	Don't Care 2	Value of 0100H	Don't Care 4	Value of 10XXH	Value of XX10H	ASCII DEST NAME 16	ASCII SOURCE NAME 16	...

PREV NET CONN ID 2	RETRANSMIT COUNT 2	SOURCE NODE CONNECTION ID 2	DEST ID 6	SOURCE ID 6	...

PREV NODE ID 6	CRC 4	END-OF-FRAME Value of 7EH

Figure 3-5: Name Query Packet

START DEL 7EH	DEST ADDR 6	SOURCE ADDR 6	LENGTH 2	Value of 0040H	00-07H=No Poll 80-0FH=Send Return Packet	# of packets willing to accept 0?H	CONNECTION ID 2	...

Sess. Seq. # 1	ACK Seq. # 1	Value of 0001H	Response Packet Size 2	Value of 0000H	Value of 1010H	ASCII SOURCE NAME 16	ASCII DEST NAME 16	...

DEST NODE CONNECTION ID 2	CRC 4	END-OF-FRAME Value of 7EH

Figure 3-6: Session Request Packet

START DEL 7EH	DEST ADDR 6	SOURCE ADDR 6	LENGTH 2	Value of 0040H	00-07H=No Poll 80-0FH=Send Return Packet	# of packets willing to accept 0?H	CONNECTION ID 2	•••

Sess. Seq. # 1	ACK Seq. # 1	Value of 0002H	Response Packet Size 2	DEST NODE CONNECTION ID 2	CRC 4	END-OF-FRAME Value of 7EH

Figure 3-7: Session Accept Packet

session_established flag is set in the session table, the local session number (LSN) is set, and the appropriate status is returned to the application. If it is a LISTEN ANY request, then any "session request" packet will satisfy the request.

HANG UP

If the requested session number is legal and the session is "open," NETBIOS will terminate any RECEIVE commands and then terminate the session. If a SEND command is pending, then NETBIOS waits until the SEND command has completed or timed-out.

SEND/CHAIN SEND

If the session number is legal and the session is "open," then NETBIOS sends the session data packet (Figure 3-8) as pointed at by NCB_BUFFER@ to the destination node and waits for an acknowledgment packet (Figure 3-9) or times-out and returns the appropriate status to the application.

RECEIVE/RECEIVE ANY

If the session number is legal and the session is "open," then NETBIOS will wait for a specific (name) session message for the duration of the receive packet time-out set by the application. If a session packet is received within the time-out interval, then an acknowledgment is sent back to the source and the data is transferred to the buffer pointed at by NCB_BUFFER@. NETBIOS also checks to ensure that the length of the received message is not greater than the buffer length (set by NCB_LENGTH). The operation of RECEIVE ANY is similar except that reception can be from any name.

36

START DEL 7EH	DEST ADDR 6	SOURCE ADDR 6	LENGTH 2	Value of 4000H	00-07H=No Poll 08-0FH=Send Return Packet	# of packets willing to accept 0?H	CONNECTION ID 2	•••

Sess. Seq. # 1	ACK Seq. # 1	80-F0H = End of Message	DATA FIELD Variable Length	•••

DEST NODE CONNECTION ID 2	CRC 4	END-OF-FRAME Value of 7EH

Figure 3-8: Session Data Packet

START DEL 7EH	DEST ADDR 6	SOURCE ADDR 6	LENGTH 2	Value of 4000H	40-47H=No Poll 48-4FH=Send Return Packet	# of packets willing to accept 0?H	CONNECTION ID 2	•••

Sess. Seq. # 1	ACK Seq. # 1	Don't Care 1	DEST NODE CONNECTION ID 2	CRC 4	END-OF-FRAME Value of 7EH

Figure 3-9: Acknowledgment Packet

SEND DATAGRAM/SEND BROADCAST DATAGRAM

For SEND DATAGRAM, NETBIOS checks the requested name number against a match in the name table. If a match is found, NETBIOS sends the datagram packet (Figure 3-10) to the destination node. For a BROADCAST, the name number is checked, and if valid, the datagram is broadcast to all nodes on the network. The datagram is sent only once, with the address field at the data link level set to all ones.

START DEL 7EH	DEST ADDR 6	SOURCE ADDR 6	LENGTH 2	Value of 5100H	Value of 0100H	Value of 0001H	Value of 1010H	Value of 0000H	
									•••

ASCII SOURCE NAME 16	ASCII DEST NAME 16	DATA FIELD Variable Length	RETRANSMIT COUNT 2	
				•••

SOURCE NODE CONNECTION ID 2	DEST ID 6	SOURCE ID 6	PREV NODE ID 6	CRC 4	END-OF-FRAME Value of 7EH

Figure 3-10: Datagram Packet

RECEIVE DATAGRAM/RECEIVE BROADCAST DATAGRAM

If the name number is found in the local name table, then NETBIOS waits for the arrival of a datagram (other than broadcast). The application can designate a specific name from which to receive a datagram or else "any". If a datagram is received, but it is not from the name the application had requested, then NETBIOS continues to wait. If the application wants any datagram, then NETBIOS returns to the application. In both cases, the received message is copied to the NCB_BUFFER@, and the local name number of the received datagram is returned to the application. RECEIVE BROADCAST DATAGRAM is a specific case that watches for a destination address of all ones.

3.3 Transport Layer

The session layer calls on the transport layer to establish a reliable connection between two names (source and destination PCs). NETBIOS tries up to a maximum number of times to make the connection. If an ack (Figure 3-9) is received, then the connection is successful. From then on, in the case of PC Network, the reliable stream protocol (RSP) is used. The RSP protocol is highly proprietary in the PC Network, and other NETBIOS implementations undoubtedly use some other protocol such as Xerox Network Systems (XNS), the Transmission Control Protocol (TCP), or the ISO/NBS transport level protocols.

3.4 Network Layer

The network layer on the IBM PC Network uses the packet transfer protocol (PTP). PTP consists of four major procedures: send PTP packet, send link access protocol (LAP) frame, receive LAP frame, and received frame.

The send PTP procedure requests that a buffer be sent to a specific network connection ID. If a connection exists, then the buffer is formatted and sent via a LAP frame. Note that even though this protocol/procedure allows internetworking to be implemented, the IBM PC Network NETBIOS implementation allows a packet to be passed to only one other network (adapter).

The send LAP frame procedure sends a buffer to a specified destination node or broadcast address by passing a properly formatted request to the data link layer. The receive LAP frame procedure receives valid frames directly from the data link layer. This procedure is also responsible for allocating and deallocating buffers as frames are received.

If a frame is received from the previous procedure, then the received frame procedure is invoked. This procedure checks the packet type for one of the following: connection data; route completion; discovery; datagram; route establishment; or a duplicate (which is ignored). Datagrams are passed to the transport layer for further processing. Datagrams are the lowest form of packet in the network, and all higher level protocols including the NETBIOS SEND commands, eventually use them indirectly in a chain of events (session to transport to network to data link).

Chapter 4 - Server Message Block (SMB) Protocol

> Functional description of the Server Message Block (SMB)
> File access protocols
> Print server protocols
> Message protocols

4.1 Overview

The Server Message Block (SMB) protocol is implemented by the redirector and server functions of the IBM PC Network Program. SMB operates at the application level, and the IBM version requires NETBIOS for proper operation. SMB is designed to be machine- and operating system-independent, although the IBM implementation is closely tied to PC-DOS.

While SMB is an "open" protocol as published by IBM, few vendors have chosen to implement it in their PC LANs. One third-party vendor, 3Com Corporation, has decided to use it in its 3+ implementation. One reason for this choice is that 3Com and AT&T have an OEM agreement whereby AT&T bundles the 3Com software with its STARLAN 1 Mbps baseband LAN for small AT&T (6300 and 7300) computers. Other vendors, such as Novell, have implemented their own "redirector" (the shell) and server protocols for reasons of efficiency and added functionality.

The IBM PC LAN program can be broken up into four major functions: redirector, receiver, messenger, and server. The redirector intercepts DOS 21H function calls and determines whether the request is for a local device or a remote device. If the device is local, the redirector simply passes the request to the local operating system (DOS 3.1 or greater for the IBM PC Network, DOS 3.2 or greater for the Token-Ring). If the request is for a remote device, then the redirector must translate it into SMB protocols.

The receiver listens for SMB protocols passed from another PC on the network, then removes a message portion that is human-readable and passes it to a local device such as the screen, a file, or a printer.

The messenger is a superset of the receiver; in addition to handling messages, it can also send messages the other way. In other words, it can translate messages from the user into SMB to be sent off over the network to another PC.

The server is the most complex function of the program in that it implements the full set of SMB protocols and manages local devices for shared use by other PCs on the network. Types of requests that it must handle from the other PCs include requests to access files and print spooling.

The first three functions -- redirector, receiver, and messenger --- can also be viewed as a subset of the server. Information exchanges are always initiated by an action from a requester PC. The requester is usually the redirector, and the request is sent to one of the four configurations as described above. Handshaking is established and information is exchanged.

4.2 Naming

Naming is key to supporting communication between two points on the network. SMB supports two classes of names: network names and network paths.

Network names are 16-byte character strings that form the machine, server, redirector, main user, and additional user names added to a local name table of each PC. The names themselves can be up to 15 bytes long; if necessary, they are padded with blanks. A one- byte suffix is added to identify the type.

A machine name is an up-to-15 character name given to the computer by the configuring software, under the control of the end user. A server name is a 16-byte name consisting of the machine name with a 20H in the sixteenth byte. This name is used in a workstation PC to communicate with a server PC. A redirector name is a 16-byte name consisting of the machine name with a 00H in the sixteenth byte. It is used to communicate with the redirector. The additional user name consists of the machine name with a 03H in the sixteenth byte. Its main purpose is to send and receive messages. A forwarded name is a user, main, or additional name whose sixteenth byte has been changed to 05H.

Network path names are associated with resources that are to be shared. For each resource, such as a subdirectory on a server's hard disk, a network path name is created for the subdirectory (path) by prefixing the machine name to the resource (path) name.

A network path name has the following format:

\\nnnnnnnnnnnnnnn\dddddddd...ddd

where nnn...n is a 1 to 15 character machine name and ddd...d is a device name or directory path. The maximum network path length is 146 bytes.

4.3 Establishing a PC-to-Server Connection

When a user attempts to "connect" to the resources of a server (such as via the PC LAN Program NET USE command), the redirector attempts to establish a session with the server. If there is room in the local adapter's address table, then a session is started in which the redirector and server agree upon a protocol and start communicating.

On the server side, the redirector requests that a connection be set up to the resource to be shared (such as the subdirectory in the example above). The server will make sure that the requested resource exists, and if so, check the optional password for validity. The server then responds with a maximum server transmission block size and a connection handle called the network path ID (similar to the handle returned by PC-DOS when opening a file) to be used for all future requests to the resources. When the connection is terminated, the redirector tells the server to end the connection and free the handle.

A user may request that messages be forwarded to another computer. If this is the case, then the sender (such as a server) requests that the target computer add the user name to the network as a forwarded name. From then on, the messages for that user will go to the target computer.

4.4 The SMB Protocols

The SMB protocol set consists of four types of server message blocks: session (connection) control, file, printer, and message. Session control fulfills two major functions: dialect determination and connection control.

Given that the PC LAN Program is in operation (and thus the SMB protocols are in effect), once a session is established between a redirector PC and a server PC, the redirector sends the command VERIFY DIALECT with a list of supported dialects back to the server. The server then determines if it can support one of the dialects. If so, it sends back to the redirector an indication of which dialect will be used. If the server cannot support any of the dialects, it sends an error response back to the redirector PC and the session is terminated; otherwise, communication may commence.

Connection control consists of commands which start and end a redirector connection to a shared resource at the server. The START CONNECTION command establishes the connection between a redirector PC and a shared resource at a server PC. All further commands and responses use this session. The END CONNECTION command terminates the connection between the redirector and the shared resource.

Once a connection is established via the START CONNECTION command, the redirector may use the file access commands to access files at the server. These commands are similar to the local PC-DOS function calls which allow access to files and directory. Additional commands have been added to determine the configuration and status of the remote shared resources. The supported file access commands include: check, create, and remove directories; create file, create temporary file, create new file; delete or rename file; get or set file attributes, search multiple files and get disk attributes; open and close files; read and write a byte block; commit process and end process; and finally, lock and unlock a byte block.

The print server commands allow a redirector to send files to a print queue at a server and obtain status information about the print queue. Commands include create spool file, spool byte block, close spool file, and return print queue.

The message commands are used to send and receive messages. They include commands to send and receive short messages (one transmission) or long messages (multiple transmissions), to forward (or cancel) messages, and to send a broadcast message (short message only). While the message protocols allow multiple user names at one PC to send or receive messages, the IBM PC LAN Program implementation allows messages to be sent only from a single name. The commands that support messages include send single block message, send broadcast message, send start of multiple block message, send text of multiple block message, send end of multiple block message, forward user name, cancel forward, and get machine name.

SMB Format

The generic SMB fields and structure (format) are described in this section. This is followed by a brief description of each SMB command. Note that the terms "device name," "dirname," and "file name" refer to their PC-DOS equivalents (e.g., a device name such as PRN:). A dialect name is a string of characters with the same restrictions as a file name (8 characters plus an optional 3- character extension). The network name and network path names are structured as discussed at the beginning of this chapter. An origin and destination name is a 1-to-15-character machine name (also discussed earlier). A password is a 1-to-8-character name with the same restrictions as a PC-DOS file name.

Figure 4-1 illustrates the generic SMB format.

FIELD	SIZE	DESCRIPTION
SMB_ID	DB 0FFH	PC Network Program 1.0 Message Type
SMB_SERVER	DB 'SMB'	SMB Server Type
SMB_FUNCTION	DB 0	Function Code
SME RET_CLASS	DB 0	Return Error Class
SMB_HEINFO	DB 0	AH value on INT 24H or reserved = 0
SMB_RETCODE	DW 0	Return Error Code
SMB_RESV1	DB 0	Reserved; must be 0
SMB_RESV2	DB 0	Reserved; must be 0
SMB_RESV8	DW 0	Reserved; must be 0
SMB_NPID	DW 0	Network Path ID
SMB_PID	DW 0	Process ID
SMB_RESV9	DW 0	Reserved; must be 0
SMB_RES10	DW 0	Reserved; must be 0
SMB_PARMCNT	DB 0	Count of Parameters in SMB
SMB_P1-PN	DW 0	SMB Function Dependent Parameters
SMB_BUFLEN	DW 0	Length of SMB_BUF
SMB_BUF	DB 'bytes'	Start of SMB_BUF area

Figure 4-1: Server Message Block (SMB) Generic Format

The SMB_FUNCTION field can take on the follow values:

Value   Meaning

00H   Create directory
01H   Delete directory

02H   Open file
03H   Create file
04H   Close file
05H   Commit all files
06H   Delete file
07H   Rename file
08H   Get file attribute
09H   Set file attribute

0AH	Read byte block
0BH	Write byte block
0CH	Lock byte block
0DH	Unlock byte block
0EH	Create unique file
0FH	Create new file
10H	Check directory
11H	End of process
12H	LSEEK
70H	Start connection
71H	End connection
72H	Verify dialect
80H	Get disk attributes
81H	Search multiple files
C0H	Create spool file
C1H	Spool byte block
C2H	Close spool file
C3H	Return print queue
D0H	Send message
D1H	Send broadcast
D2H	Forward user name
D3H	Cancel forward
D4H	Get machine name
D5H	Start multi-block message
D6H	End multi-block message
D7H	Multi-block message text

The SMB_RETCODE field can take on the following values (with SMB_RETCLASS = 00H):

Value	Meaning
0054H	Message has been buffered
0055H	Message has been logged
0056H	User message displayed

The SMB_RETCODE field can take on the following values (with SMB_RETCLASS = 02H):

Value   Meaning

0000H   Reserved
0001H   Unknown error
0002H   Bad password
0003H   Device type mismatch on assign
0004H   Netname access level violated
0005H   Invalid network path ID
0006H   Network path not found
0007H   Invalid device

0031H   Print queue full (number of files)
0032H   Print queue out of space
0033H   End of file on print queue dump
0034H   Invalid print file ID

0051H   Server is paused
0052H   Not receiving messages
0053H   No room to buffer message
0057H   Too many remote user names
0058H   Duplicate name on network

FFFFH   Function not supported

Session Control Commands

VERIFY DIALECT - This command is sent by the redirector to the server to establish the dialect to be used. Currently only one dialect is supported by the PC Network Program.

START CONNECTION - This command establishes a connection between the redirector and the server shared resource. The server contains a table that maps the shared resource from the network path name to the local name, the type of resource, and an optional password. The server returns a network path ID that must be used for subsequent requests for that resource. Start connection can also be used for PC-to-PC communication in which the maximum transmission size is assumed to be 512 bytes.

File Commands

CREATE DIRECTORY - Sent from redirector to server to perform the PC-DOS MKDIR (make directory) function.

REMOVE DIRECTORY - Sent from redirector to server to perform the PC-DOS RMDIR (remove directory) function.

CHECK DIRECTORY - Sent by the redirector to determine if a directory at the server exists when a user does a DOS CHDIR (check directory) command.

OPEN FILE - Sent by the redirector to a server to open a file and return the file handle (just like the local PC-DOS operation). Starting with PC-DOS 3.0, a number of additional file open modes were added to support multi-user environments. The various modes are described in the following table:

File Open Mode	Meaning
Compatibility	Provides compatibility with applications which used previous versions of PC-DOS. A file may be opened any number of times, provided that it is not opened in one of the PC-DOS 3.0 and higher modes.
Deny Read/Write	Used to gain exclusive access to the file. The request is rejected if the file is already open in any other mode.
Deny Write	Allows the file to be opened as many times as requested for reading. The request is rejected if the file has been opened with a write access or in compatibility mode.
Deny Read	Allows the file to be opened for writing. The request is rejected if the file has already been opened for reading in compatibility mode.
Deny None	Allows the file to be opened as many times as requested for read/write. The request is rejected if the file is already open in any other mode.

If an application opens a file using the File Control Block (FCB) method via DOS INT 21H, function 0FH, then the sharing modes are not supported.

Figure 4-2 summarizes the various file modes and accesses.

1st File Open Mode / 2nd and Subsequent File Open Attempts

1st File Open Mode		Deny Read/Write			Deny Write			Deny Read			Allow Read/Write		
		Input	Input/Output	Output	Input	Input/Output	Output	Input	Input/Output	Output	Input	Input/Output	Output
Deny Read/Write	Input												
	Input/Output												
	Output												
Deny Write	Input				▨						▨		
	Input/Output										▨		
	Output							▨			▨		
Deny Read	Input					▨							▨
	Input/Output												▨
	Output									▨			
Allow Read/Write	Input				▨	▨					▨	▨	▨
	Input/Output										▨	▨	▨
	Output							▨	▨	▨	▨	▨	▨

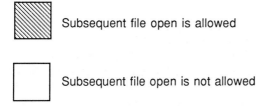

▨ Subsequent file open is allowed

☐ Subsequent file open is not allowed

Figure 4-2: File Modes and Accesses

CREATE FILE - Sent by the redirector to a server to create a new file and return a handle. It may also be used to effectively delete an old file and create a new one with the same name. The request is rejected if the file is open or the file attribute is set to read only.

CLOSE FILE - Sent by the redirector to a server to close a file. The redirector must send the file handle.

COMMIT FILE - Sent by the redirector to a server to request that all buffers for a file be written to the server's hard disk. The redirector specifies a file handle, and the server responds when the operation is complete. Multiple files may be "committed" if the redirector specifies that all files opened in the connection represented by the network path ID in the SMB_NPID field be committed.

DELETE FILE - Sent by the redirector to a server to delete a file. The redirector specifies the file handle. The request is rejected if a file is open or marked as read only.

RENAME FILE - Sent by the redirector to a server to rename a file.

GET FILE ATTRIBUTES - Sent by the redirector to the server to obtain the file's attributes, time of last access, and size.

SET FILE ATTRIBUTES - Sent by the redirector to the server to set file attributes.

READ BYTE BLOCK - Sent by the redirector to the server to read a block of data from a file.

WRITE BYTE BLOCK - The complement of READ BYTE BLOCK; sent by the redirector to the server to write a block of data from a file.

LSEEK - LSEEK stands for Long Seek, which is sent to the server to move the file pointer. The PC LAN Program uses this function to determine the size of a file. The file must have been previously opened in a mode that supports shared read.

LOCK BYTE BLOCK - Supports the extended file byte-range locking function of PC-DOS 3.0 and higher. Sent by the redirector to the server to lock a region of bytes within a file. The region can be from one byte to the entire file. The request is rejected if any byte overlaps a region already locked. Note that this function does not adequately support transaction processing insofar as atomic locks (multiple lock requests in a single request to perform a transaction) are not supported. Some servers, such as Novell's NetWare, support atomic locks.

UNLOCK BYTE BLOCK - Complement of LOCK BYTE BLOCK; sent by the redirector to the server to unlock a region of bytes within a file.

CREATE UNIQUE FILE - Sent by the redirector to the server to request that a unique file name be generated by the server (actually PC-DOS running at that server). The server then returns this unique name to the redirector. Unique name requests are used by many applications that require temporary work files.

CREATE NEW FILE - Similar to Create Unique File, except that the file name must be unique to files already in that directory.

END OF PROCESS - Sent by the redirector to the server to terminate work within a connection. It is sent for each network path a redirector has active.

GET DISK ATTRIBUTES - Sent by the redirector to the server to get information about hard disk storage size and layout.

SEARCH MULTIPLE FILES - Sent by the redirector to the server to perform the PC-DOS FCB and ASCIIZ search functions. The path and file name is passed to the server. The search can also check for hidden and system files.

Print Commands

CREATE SPOOL FILE - Sent by the redirector to the server to set up a data stream in which to spool print data.

SPOOL BYTE BLOCK - Sent by the redirector to the server to spool a block of data from a file. The first block sent contains set-up information for the printer.

CLOSE SPOOL FILE - Sent by the redirector to the server to close (mark to end of) a print spool. The server then queues the file for printing.

RETURN PRINT QUEUE - Sent by the redirector to the server to return the contents of the server print queue.

Message Commands

SEND SINGLE BLOCK MESSAGE - Sent from one redirector to another, sends a short (single block) message consisting of a maximum of 128 characters (a PC Network Program limitation).

SEND BROADCAST MESSAGE - Sends a short message to all receivers on the network. A broadcast message is sent as a datagram; thus there are no responses from the receivers.

SEND START OF MULTI-BlOCK MESSAGE - Sent by a sender to start a message of multiple blocks. The receiver returns a message group ID to be used for subsequent message blocks.

SEND TEXT OF MULTI-BLOCK MESSAGE - Sent by a sender to send a message of up to 1,600 characters in 128-character blocks.

SEND END OF MULTI-BLOCK MESSAGE - Sent by a sender to indicate the end of a multiple block message.

FORWARD USER NAME - Sent by a sender to a server (or subset) requesting that the server receive messages for an additional user name. There must be room in the server's table to add the name.

CANCEL FORWARD - Complement of FORWARD USER NAME. The server (or subset will delete the name from its table.

GET MACHINE NAME - Sent to get the machine name of a user name. This command is usually used in conjunction with CANCEL FORWARD in order to get the name to which to send the CANCEL FORWARD command.

Chapter 5 - Other Vendor Implementations

Non-IBM implementations of NETBIOS
AST Research
Excelan
Novell
The Software Link
Protocol Analyzers
Network General

5.1 Non-IBM Implementations of NETBIOS

This chapter describes the NETBIOS implementations of four vendors. One implementation is from a PC board manufacturer, another is from an Ethernet front-end board manufacturer, the third is from a PC LAN file server software vendor, and the fourth is from a multi-user software vendor. Common to all vendors is a NETBIOS-compatible session level interface that conforms to the NETBIOS 5CH interrupt function calls and results returned. What differs from vendor to vendor is the underlying protocols that are used to implement the layers below the session layer (Layer 5), namely the transport and network layers. In many cases, the network layer interfaces to a particular type of data link layer; thus, the particular NETBIOS implementation really only runs on that vendor's network technology, despite the "portability" of high-level protocols, including NETBIOS. It should be noted, however, that all vendors are open to porting their intermediate protocols to other LAN technology; thus users could implement the NETBIOS emulator of their liking on the underlying LAN technology of their choice.

AST Research

The AST Research (Irvine, CA) NETBIOS option fully implements all NETBIOS functions, allowing the IBM PC LAN Program or other NETBIOS-compatible applications to operate properly. Large portions of it were written in "C", making it somewhat portable. It is available for AST's PCnet, PCnet-II, and RSN. AST is also willing to sell it to OEMs for customization. The underlying protocols used are based on XNS.

The AST implementation allows the user more control over the operation of NETBIOS than other implementations, including IBM's. When configuring the software, the user can accept the defaults or optionally specify the CALL, NAME, SESSION, and ACK time-out value, the NAME, SEND, SESSION, and DATAGRAM retry count, the number of open sessions, the number of outstanding commands, and adjustable data packet sizes.

The general implementation of AST's NETBIOS is illustrated in Figure 5-1.

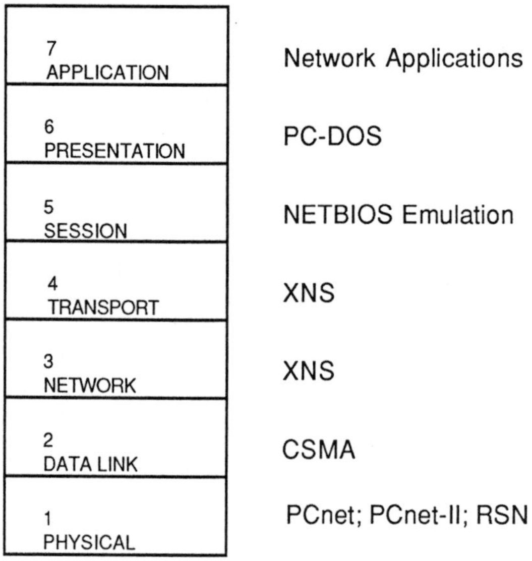

7 APPLICATION	Network Applications
6 PRESENTATION	PC-DOS
5 SESSION	NETBIOS Emulation
4 TRANSPORT	XNS
3 NETWORK	XNS
2 DATA LINK	CSMA
1 PHYSICAL	PCnet; PCnet-II; RSN

Figure 5-1: AST Research NETBIOS Implementation

Excelan

Excelan, Inc. (San Jose, CA) has a NETBIOS emulator for end users that provides all of the IBM NETBIOS interrupt 5CH commands. This implementation runs on top of Excelan's TCP/IP protocols that in turn communicate over an Ethernet LAN. Excelan's OEM offering of TCP/IP protocols is designed to operate with Excelan equipment (Ethernet front-end processors). Excelan will offer OEMs a version of NETBIOS/TCP/IP that can be customized. One should note that TCP/IP implementations from multiple vendors are more compatible with each other and likely to communicate than implementations based on protocols such as Xerox Network Systems (XNS).

54

Figure 5-2 summarizes the Excelan NETBIOS implementation on Ethernet.

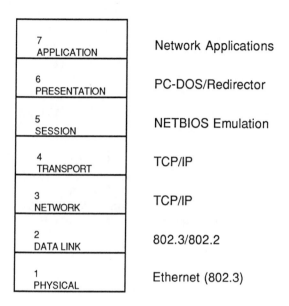

7 APPLICATION	Network Applications
6 PRESENTATION	PC-DOS/Redirector
5 SESSION	NETBIOS Emulation
4 TRANSPORT	TCP/IP
3 NETWORK	TCP/IP
2 DATA LINK	802.3/802.2
1 PHYSICAL	Ethernet (802.3)

Figure 5-2: Excelan NETBIOS Implementation

Novell

Novell, Inc. (Orem, UT) added full NETBIOS emulation to Version 2.01 of Advanced NetWare. Full IBM NETBIOS interrupt 5CH commands are supported in the workstation, and are recognized by the server. In fact, both Novell and IBM servers (via the IBM PC Local Area Network Program) can operate simultaneously, and a workstation operating either the Novell shell or the IBM PC LAN Program can access a Novell server. Of course, a workstation running the Novell shell can access only the Novell server and not a PC configured as a server under the IBM PC LAN Program.

The Novell implementation operates on top of Novell's IPX (Internet Packet eXchange) protocols. The implementation thus gives users NETBIOS compatibility with any of the two dozen or so PC LANs supported by Advanced NetWare (including PC Network), as well as improved performance. It is interesting to note that tests conducted by Novell have shown a factor of 2 better performance in end-to-end workstation throughput using the emulator over the native NETBIOS in PC Network. The user can specify which NETBIOS to use when installing the workstation shell.

Another technique implemented by Novell to improve performance reduces the overhead associated with passing packets between layers. With NETBIOS, packets are processed such that each layer adds its own pieces of information as packets are passed through. For example, when the transport layer receives a packet from the session layer (NETBIOS), it is copied into a larger buffer where the transport protocols can add its headers and trailers. Layer protocols and interactions must be implemented in strict adherence to the OSI Reference Model. In theory, only packets are passed between layers, not information about buffer and work areas used by another layer. This promotes interoperability and compatibility with other vendors' implementations of a particular protocol.

In Novell's implementation, packets are not sent from NETBIOS (at the session layer) to the transport layer. Instead, a pointer is passed from one layer to the next, thus reducing processor and bus overhead from redundant copying. This streamlines the process but violates the "spirit" of the OSI model. Many other vendors also use this technique for performance and competitive reasons.

Figure 5-3 illustrates the Novell NETBIOS implementation for NetWare-supported PC LANs. Also note that Novell has implemented its own version of Microsoft's redirector.

7 APPLICATION	Network Applications
6 PRESENTATION	PC-DOS/Shell
5 SESSION	NETBIOS Emulation
4 TRANSPORT	IPX
3 NETWORK	IPX
2 DATA LINK	CSMA/Token-Bus/Token-Ring
1 PHYSICAL	Most major PC LANs

Figure 5-3: Novell NETBIOS Implementation

The Software Link

Unlink the three vendors discussed previously, The Software Link (Atlanta, GA) has developed a NETBIOS emulator for non-LAN products. The company has developed two products to allow users of IBM PCs to share resources (printers and hard disks).

The first product turns a PC or AT into a multi-user, multi- tasking machine. Multilink Advanced partitions RAM to concurrently run up to nine applications. As many as eight ASCII terminals (including The Software Link's Shadow, a terminal with IBM keyboard and screen emulation) may be connected to the host PC via RS-232 ports.

The second product, LANlink, allows one to configure a low-level network consisting of interconnected PCs in a star configuration. Stars can connect to other stars as well as to remote PCs, allowing a fairly arbitrary topology. Unlike with Multilink Advanced, PCs are attached to the host, not terminals. As with Multilink Advanced, RS- 232 ports are used; however, the ports are driven at 56 Kbps with a proprietary data-compression technique that gives an effective throughput of 115 Kbps. The "satellite" PCs connect to a "server" PC and can use the server's hard disk as a local virtual drive (as in a PC LAN environment).

Both products can run all applications that are PC DOS 3.1 and/or NETBIOS compatible. Figure 5-4 illustrates the implementation of NETBIOS by The Software Link for LANlink.

Other Vendors

Many other vendors offer a NETBIOS option for their networks. They also take the approaches discussed above; in other words, they provide a 5CH session layer emulator and use the transport and network protocols of their choice. There are minor differences between the vendors in terms of enhancements (at the cost of downward compatibility to IBM's NETBIOS), and native services (e.g., Novell's shell) with which NETBIOS can co-exist in the vendor's LAN.

5.2 Protocol Analyzers

As local area networks proliferate and become more complex, the need for specialized tools has arisen. These tools can aid in diagnostics, debugging, maintenance, management, and administration of a network.

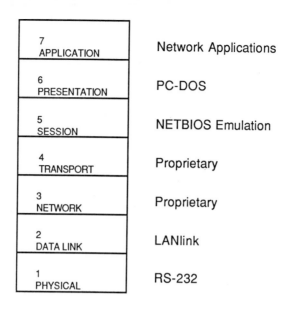

Layer	OSI	Implementation
7	APPLICATION	Network Applications
6	PRESENTATION	PC-DOS
5	SESSION	NETBIOS Emulation
4	TRANSPORT	Proprietary
3	NETWORK	Proprietary
2	DATA LINK	LANlink
1	PHYSICAL	RS-232

Figure 5-4: The Software Link NETBIOS Implementation

The first available LAN tools were those that gathered statistics about a network's performance (e.g., network loading, packets per second throughput) and health (e.g., CRC errors, collisions, lost tokens). These tools monitored primarily the data link layer within the LAN.

The second category of tools to become available sat on top of the LAN systems software to allow a manager to control the operation of the network. With these tools, the manager could control user access to network nodes and the ports attached to these nodes and also define various parameters under which the nodes would operate (e.g., permanent virtual circuits, terminal characteristics, flow control).

The third category of tools becoming available are those that are able to monitor the intermediate protocols -- Layers 3 through 6 (network through presentation) of the OSI Reference Model. With these tools, a manager can monitor the performance of the protocols and identify bottlenecks or trouble spots. The tools also allow developers to implement and debug protocols and ensure that they are indeed compatible with the way a certain set of protocols (such as NETBIOS) is defined.

The Sniffer

The first commercially available protocol analyzer for NETBIOS (and the only one available at the writing of this book), is The Sniffer from Network General Corporation (Sunnyvale, CA).

The Sniffer is a combination of hardware and software which serves as a data analyzer for the IBM Token-Ring. It can capture all frames transmitted on the network for analysis. It monitors the network and analyzes data in much the same way that a logic analyzer does for digital signals. The software includes real- time performance monitoring and filtering of desired packet types. For more complex event sequences, the user can custom program for certain trap conditions. All frames are timestamped and can be stored to disk for later analysis.

Another useful function of the Sniffer is its ability to inject frames into the network. This allows a manager to determine how the network will react to an increase in load. This "load analysis" can be used to determine the affects of adding more active devices to the network. "Extra" or erroneous NETBIOS packets can also be injected into the network in order to see how well a workstation or server handles them.

The types of frames that can be monitored on the Token-Ring include IEEE 802.5 Medium Access Control (MAC) frames, IEEE 802.2 Types 1 and 2 Logical Link Control (LLC) frames, all of the NETBIOS session level commands, the SMB protocols, and LU 6.2 (APPC and SNA) protocols.

The Sniffer is built around a high-performance personal computer (a portable IBM PC AT compatible running at 8 MHz), making it a useful tool both in the field and in the lab.

A tool similar to the Sniffer but intended for Ethernet LANs is the LANalyzer from Excelan. Also built around an IBM PC AT- compatible portable (from Compaq), it allows managers and users to analyze traffic on an Ethernet LAN. Direct support for monitoring NETBIOS protocols is not provided, but the software allows customization to monitor frames of a certain bit pattern. An individual with knowledge of the bit fields within NETBIOS packets could thus set up a system to monitor such packets. The LANalyzer can also be used for load analysis.

Chapter 6 - Microsoft Networks

How Microsoft Networks and NETBIOS compare
The transport control block (TCB)
Microsoft Networks' viability

6.1 Overview

When the IBM PC Network was first announced, there was a great deal of confusion in the industry as to what networking software IBM had implemented. Shortly after the IBM announcement, many LAN vendors responded by announcing support for Microsoft Networks, thinking that that was what was being used in PC Network. There was some precedent for this belief: after all, Microsoft's MS- DOS did become PC-DOS to IBM. (Microsoft Networks is strictly an OEM product. It is not implemented on any particular LAN -- that is up to the OEM.)

It wasn't until after PC Network was released that users and vendors began to realize that the networking software in PC Network (which later became known as NETBIOS) was incompatible with Microsoft Networks and not written by Microsoft. As a result, a flood of Microsoft Networks-compatible products announced from many LAN vendors never materialized.

Microsoft did change the Microsoft Networks' user command structure after PC Network was released in order to closely correspond to the commands used by IBM. (For example, the CONNECT command became NET USE.) In fact, the Microsoft Networks commands are essentially a subset of those used in the IBM PC LAN Program.

Only one component of IBM's NETBIOS implementation was actually written by Microsoft. That component is the redirector. The redirector has close ties to PC/MS-DOS, even though the rest of Microsoft Networks and NETBIOS is designed to be both operating system- and LAN-independent. In fact, Microsoft Networks is available for both Xenix (Microsoft's implementation of UNIX, System V) and MS-DOS. The redirector is responsible for ensuring that requests for services (such as opening or printing files), which are normally handled locally, are, if necessary, intercepted, transformed into a network request, and sent to a server for execution.

Like NETBIOS, Microsoft Networks is designed to work with MS-DOS 3.1 (both workstation and server rely on it) or higher. File- sharing modes and file locking are identical. The extended naming scheme is also the same (\\server_name\ directory\file).

6.2 Microsoft Networks vs. NETBIOS

The key difference between Microsoft Networks and NETBIOS is that Microsoft Networks provides a transport-level interface, while the NETBIOS interface is at the session level (see Figure 6-1). Microsoft Networks also includes dedicated server and workstation software, while the IBM PC LAN program, which provides these and other functions, must be purchased separately for the IBM PC Network or Token-Ring.

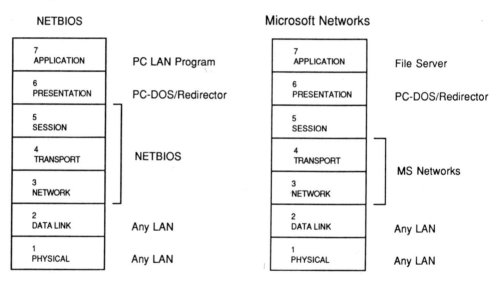

Figure 6-1: NETBIOS vs. Microsoft Networks

Microsoft Networks' transport layer is used to send messages reliably via virtual circuits. Up to 64K bytes can be sent per request. Communication with the transport layer is via interrupt 21H, function 5BH (recalled that NETBIOS uses interrupt 21H, function 5CH).

Communication with the transport layer is accomplished by setting up a transport control block (TCB), then performing the 21H interrupt. The transport control block is analogous to setting up a NCB or MCB in NETBIOS. In fact, many fields are common to both the TCB and NCB/MCB implementation. Figure 6-2 shows the structure of the transport control block.

Field Name	Length (in bytes) and Meaning	
COMMAND	1	- COMMAND FIELD
CID	1	- COMMAND ID
VCID	1	- VIRCUIT CIRCUIT ID-NUMBER
LENGTH	2	- DATA BUFFER SIZE
BADDR	4	- POINTER TO MESSAGE BUFFER ADDRESS (OFFSET:SEGMENT)
RES1	2	- RESERVED
LADDR	16	- LOCAL ADDRESS
RADDR	16	- REMOTE ADDRESS
ASYNC	4	- POINTER TO ADDRESS NOTIFICATION ROUTINE (OFFSET:SEGMENT)
LNET	4	- LOCAL LAN NUMBER
RNET	4	- REMOTE LAN NUMBER
RTO	1	- RECIEVE TIME-OUT (500 MS INCREMENT)
STO	1	- SEND TIME-OUT (500 MS INCREMENT)
RES2	8	- RESERVED

Figure 6-2: Transport Control Block (TCB)

As with NETBIOS, the network layer in Microsoft Networks is only minimally implemented. Included is support for a hierarchical address consisting of a 4-byte network address and a 16-byte station address. Also included is low-level support for datagram service allowing unreliable (unacknowledged) packets of up to 512 bytes to be sent/received. The OEM must determine how to map the station addresses into a network address and how to implement a routing algorithm if a gateway is to be implemented.

Unfortunately, there are many differences between Microsoft Networks and NETBIOS which make compatibility somewhat difficult. For example, in addition to the differences pointed out above, the two naming schemes are incompatible. NETBIOS allows multiple names, dynamic reassignment, and forwarding of names; whereas MS Networks requires that an administrator assign one logical name to each physical address. Yet another "quirk" with MS Networks is that should a workstation that set a file lock fail, it alone can release the lock after rebooting; otherwise, the server must be rebooted to clear the lock!

While the two implementations differ, they suffer from one common fault: both rely on MS/PC-DOS to carry out services to the file server. In other words, they are both tied into the deficiencies of this single-user, single-tasking operating system. It is not even clear that a multi-tasking version of DOS would resolve the problem, since in order to perform well, it more than likely would not be compatible with previous DOS versions, leaving five million PC owners up in arms.

Some of the LAN vendors that announced support for Microsoft Networks have actually shipped production versions for their networks. Ironically, many of them are now offering NETBIOS as well. It appears that Microsoft Networks' usefulness in straight MS-DOS environments will be somewhat limited. Where Microsoft Networks will be useful is in LANs with a combination of Xenix and MS-DOS operating systems.

Appendix A: NETBIOS Guidelines

Introduction

Distributed systems on PC LANs require the design of high-level application-specific protocols between client and server programs. These protocols must be built upon the set of network services provided at the interface between a PC or server and its attachment to the LAN. The NETBIOS interface between a PC and a LAN has been defined by IBM and is now accepted as an important standard within the PC LAN industry. This appendix is based on information provided by Gregory Ennis of Sytek, Inc. It presents some suggested guidelines for the use of NETBIOS services.

NETBIOS Applications

Many of the existing "networked" PC software packages are basically stand-alone applications which have been modified to allow data files to be stored on a file server (i.e., on a logical drive which has been redirected to a file server). Such applications were not designed initially with a network in mind, and in fact, many will operate in this fashion without modification. These single-user applications can be further extended into the multi-user domain by taking advantage of file- and record-locking mechanisms such as those provided by DOS 3.1.

New PC applications are emerging which have been designed right from the start with a network point of view. These applications are typically multi-user and involve actual processing on multiple nodes, usually split between the user station (where a "client program" executes on behalf of the actual user) and a server station (where a corresponding server program executes). These can be thought of as protocol-based applications: an application-specific program executes in the server and communicates with the client programs through an application-specific protocol. The server is "intelligent" with respect to this particular application, since it handles not just generic file system requests but specific application-oriented commands.

In the case of personal computers attached to a NETBIOS local network, the client and server programs within a protocol-based application make direct use of NETBIOS calls. Protocol-based applications in the case of a NETBIOS network will thus be referred to as a "NETBIOS application," reflecting the fact that it is the underlying NETBIOS services which are used to support the application-specific protocol between client and server.

Application Examples

By looking at examples of NETBIOS applications, some typical architectural problems faced by the designer can be identified. Guidelines for the design of NETBIOS applications will then be presented in the following section.

Example 1: Gateways to Other Networks

Consider a PC LAN which is to be connected to another network. This may be a wide-area network, such as Telenet, accessed through X.25, an SNA-based mainframe network, or even the public telephone system. To connect LAN-based PCs to such a network requires a gateway device attached to both networks, and software within the user's PC which knows how to communicate with the gateway and with the other network. The combination of the gateway and the software within the user PC forms a protocol-based application, with the gateway playing the role of server. If the LAN supports NETBIOS, the client program within the user PC and the gateway server program can communicate via a protocol built on top of NETBIOS services.

The designer of such a NETBIOS-based gateway application must decide how to use the specific NETBIOS services. The following issues must be addressed:

- What NETBIOS names are to be used?

- What is the relationship between the names used for the NETBIOS communication and the names or addresses of the actual target destination on the external network?

- How can multiple gateways be accommodated? How can they be identified?

- How can the gateway provide access to a limited number of outside connections to a larger number of potential users in a fair fashion? (In other words, how is "port contention" handled?)

Before any real communication can occur between the client and server programs of this gateway application, there must be a name registered by the gateway which is known by the client. Such a name can be registered as exclusive or non-exclusive. If the gateway program requests the registration of a name which has already been registered exclusively by another user on the network, the request will be disallowed by NETBIOS. Consequently, the designer must determine names which can be known by both the gateway and the client programs but which will be available in practice for use on a network which may have other applications (from other vendors) also registering names.

The external network may have its own naming or addressing scheme which it uses to identify its hosts or resources. The designer of the gateway application must determine how to communicate the user's desired destination to the gateway. Can this be done via the NETBIOS names, or must some other technique for communicating names be used? If the NETBIOS names that are used signify the name of the gateway rather than the name of the ultimate destination, then a naming convention for multiple gateways must be worked out by the designer.

Example 2: Distributed Databases

Some single-user PC database systems can be adapted for the LAN environment by allowing the data to be stored on a file server. In such a system, the database program executes on the user station and accesses the data through redirection of file system calls. The server itself plays no role in this application other than its generic file service function.

More advanced database systems for PC LANs incorporate an actual database server -- a program executing within a server which performs the DBMS functions and which communicates with corresponding client programs via a high-level protocol.

In this case, the protocol between the clients and servers will likely take the form of commands and responses within a database command language (such as SQL). One advantage of the NETBIOS approach for a PC database is that it allows additional servers with a server-to-server protocol similar (if not identical to) the client-server protocol to be added, thus allowing for distributed databases.

The client programs in such a system play the role of user interfaces, formatting the user requests as appropriate and exchanging transactions with the server(s). Since the client programs do not directly access a file system, the NETBIOS-based approach is independent of any particular file system (i.e., the user workstation need not all share a common file system; they could, in fact, run under different operating systems).

The issues faced by the designer of a NETBIOS-based database system include the following:

- How should the NETBIOS naming service be used? (In many respects, the issues here are the same as those faced by the designer of the NETBIOS-based gateway, such as determining names to use which are not likely to be in use already. However, since in this case there is no external network with its own naming conventions involved, the name problems with its own naming conventions are somewhat simpler.

- Should transactions be exchanged via datagrams or via sessions? On the one hand, the request/response nature of the exchanges seems to argue for datagrams. However, each transaction will likely be part of a sequence of related transactions, perhaps involving the transfer of a large amount of data, and this seems to argue for sessions.

- How can the system be designed to support the maximum number of users at a reasonable performance level? The manner in which the system's basic design uses the NETBIOS services will have a significant impact, given that the database server's attachment to the NETBIOS network will allow only a given number of simultaneous names registered and simultaneous sessions.

The following section will present some guidelines for the design of NETBIOS-based applications which address in a generic fashion some of the issues identified in these two examples.

Guidelines for Good NETBIOS Application Design

In the above examples, some of the specific architectural problems facing the designer of a NETBIOS application were identified. Fortunately, there are some simple guidelines which can be applied in many cases to solve these design problems.

Name Usage

There are two main issue regarding the usage of NETBIOS names: format and semantics. In the absence of a centralized NETBIOS naming authority, it is necessary that the producers of NETBIOS software use common sense in choosing the format of the names to be registered. To avoid undesired conflicts with names which may already be registered on the network, it is suggested that software vendors choose a short prefix for all names which is unlikely to be chosen by another vendor (such as the first few characters of the vendor's name). As an example, IBM recommends that no names should be registered which begin with "IBM," since such names may very likely be already in use by IBM's NETBIOS applications. This convention is not 100% foolproof; consequently, applications should be designed to be able to register alternate names if necessary.

In terms of name semantics, it should be remembered that NETBIOS names are not an unlimited resource: typical NETBIOS networks allow fewer than twenty names to be registered at any one node. Names are also limited to 16 characters. Consequently, it is not likely that an application can use the NETBIOS names to signify a large number of application-specific items (such as open files, mail users, or remote destinations through a gateway). Instead, NETBIOS names are best used to identify significant functions within an application. For example, an electronic mail server might have three different names for use in communication with users, other servers, and the manager. Higher-level names (such as the names of the actual e-mail users) are then best communicated to the server via an application-specific protocol transparent to NETBIOS.

Datagram Usage

NETBIOS datagrams are not acknowledged, and they can carry only limited quantities of data. Consequently, they should be used only in those situations in which the acknowledgments, if necessary, are handled by the application protocol itself, and the data throughput requirement is low.

True broadcast datagrams can be used only in special environments which are known to have only a single application using the broadcast function (or a set of applications which are coordinated in their use of broadcasts). If a network is supporting applications from multiple vendors, it is very likely that broadcasts from one vendor's software will interfere with the other vendor's application.

Multicast datagrams to non-exclusive names can be used very effectively provided the naming guidelines stated above are followed. For example, multicast datagrams provide an effective way for a designer to accomplish system initialization functions for a multi-server application, allowing new servers to identify themselves to the system.

Session Usage

Although the name service and datagram service are important components of the NETBIOS system, it is the fundamental session service that provides application designers with their primary tool. In many applications, datagrams will be used for some initial control functions, setting up the environment and causing various names to be registered which will then be used by the sessions supporting the actual transfer of user data.

Sessions should almost always be used. Designing an application around the datagram service will typically require special reliability and fragmentation/reassembly handling within the application. The NETBIOS session service already provides these functions. The primary benefit of the datagram service is its multicast capability, and it should be used mainly in situations where that can be used to advantage.

Sessions are not a free resource--each NETBIOS interface will allow only a finite number of simultaneous sessions in a given node to be shared among possibly multiple applications. This is particularly important within a server. Consequently, application designs should include the multiplexing of several activities across a single session whenever possible (note that this may require that additional flow control functions be implemented within the application). If sessions are at a premium for a given application, they should be terminated when no longer required and re-established if needed again. This can even be done on a "least recently used" basis to efficiently share the available sessions among multiple activities.

Many server-based applications will suffer a performance degradation if the number of simultaneous clients gets too high, and it may be desirable in such a case to limit the number of simultaneous sessions allowed. Each time a new session is established, the server program can decide whether or not to post a new LISTEN to allow the next incoming session to be established. This can be used to regulate access to one-at-a-time services (such as a dial-out modem), in which case the LISTEN plays the role of a semaphore. A more sophisticated server program could dynamically decide -- on the basis of its own current loading -- whether or not to accept new sessions.

Appendix B: References

This appendix contains a list of references that the reader may wish to consult for further information on NETBIOS.

Publications from IBM

IBM has several publications and seminar proceedings relating to NETBIOS and associated services. The publications may be ordered through a local IBM sales representative or directly through IBM at 1-800-426-2468.

IBM Token-Ring Network NETBIOS Program User's Guide (6466914)

Contains information on how to load the NETBIOS program (emulator) with hard disk or working floppy diskette, configure optional parameters, display results after batch loading, and interpret the PC Network error messages. Also describes using certain programs with the NETBIOS emulator. Packaged with the NETBIOS program.

IBM Token-Ring Network/PC Network Interconnect User's Guide (6467037)

Covers configuring and reconfiguring the Interconnect program, including how to initialize Interconnect, how to receive messages from one network and forward them to another, how to check device status and monitor program activities, and how to interpret Interconnect error messages. Packaged with the Interconnect program.

IBM Token-Ring Network PC Adapter Technical Reference (6165876)

Provides technical information on the Token-Ring PC Adapter card. Contains a description of the ring media, common programming information, protocol definitions, explanation of the four interfaces (DLC, direct, NETBIOS, Adapter), commands and return codes, and Adapter card schematics.

IBM PC Network Technical Reference (6322505)

Is the original published information on NETBIOS. Includes pseudo code for all NETBIOS commands. Also contains interface details and schematics for the IBM PC Network Adapter.

IBM PC Local Area Network Program (6280083)

Accompanies the PC Local Area Network Program, which is a prerequisite to running all other NETBIOS applications. Details the installation, commands, and operation of the workstation and server configurations. Appendixes briefly describe application guidelines for developers and the programming interfaces (interrupts 2AH and 2FH).

IBM Asynchronous Communications Server Installation and Configuration Guide (SC30-3394)

Discusses loading the Asynchronous Communications Server program, providing asynchronous connections with multiple communication servers, and accessing the digital data switching capabilities of the IBM/ROLM CBX and public switched networks. Contains information on establishing outbound calls to ASCII applications from the network and accepting inbound calls destined for asynchronous communications programs running on IBM PCs. Comes with the product.

IBM Personal Computer Seminar Proceedings--IBM Asynchronous Communications Server Protocol (G320-9323)

Serves as the technical reference guide to the protocols implemented by the communications server. Functions as a guide to developing applications. Discusses the functions performed by outbound connections, inbound connections, queuing, and data transfer; includes extensive flow diagrams. Details the protocol command set and its relationship to NETBIOS.

IBM Personal Computer Seminar Proceedings--IBM PC Network Overview

Provides an overview of the IBM PC Network hardware, the NETBIOS architecture, and the PC Network Program (now the IBM PC LAN Program). Includes sufficient detail to enable readers to write applications that interface to the PC Network Program.

IBM Personal Computer Seminar Proceedings--IBM PC Network SMB Protocol

Provides detailed information and programming examples using the server message block (SMB) protocol within NETBIOS. Includes sufficient detail to enable readers to design applications that can directly communicate with each other over the Token-Ring or PC Network or perform server functions for clients.

Other References

Architecture Technology Corporation, *The Ring-Based Local Networks Report,* May 1986.

Examines the Token-Ring, IBM's strategic local area network offering, as well as the three basic kinds of ring-based LANs: slotted-ring, token-passing, and register-insertion. Also included are discussions of key vendors' products in each of these areas.

AST Research, Inc., *NETBIOS: A Key LAN Interface Standard,* August 1985.

A brief discussion of NETBIOS, Microsoft Networks, and AST's NETBIOS emulator.

Haugdahl, J. Scott, *Inside the Token-Ring,* Architecture Technology Corporation, April 1986.

Describes the Token-Ring from a technical perspective with a focus on the Token-Ring protocols, IBM's chip set vs. TI's chip set, the cabling system components, and the Token-Ring adapter handler for the IBM PC. Also includes a comparison of the Token-Ring and PC Network with a conclusion on performance.

Microsoft Corporation, *Microsoft Networks Manager's Guide* (8660- 100-0)

Covers preparing the Microsoft Networks software, testing the network, installing the network software, sharing resources, and managing and configuring the network. Appendices treat error messages, server commands, and MS-DOS system calls.

Novell, Inc., *LAN Software Report 1985,* May 1985.

Compares the components of NetWare against NETBIOS, the IBM PC Network Program, and Microsoft Networks. Also contains an excellent discussion of the features of DOS 3.1 that pertain to multi-user capability (networking).

About the Author...

J. Scott Haugdahl is a Senior Systems Specialist at Architecture Technology Corporation. His work has included simulation and performance analysis of multi-processor computer systems, design and implementation of specialized server software and protocols for personal computer local networks, design and testing of advanced hardware for servers on PC local networks, and analysis of the latest developments and product offerings in the PC local network market. He has researched, written, and presented numerous seminars on PC LANs in both the U.S. and Europe. He has also presented papers and tutorials for IEEE and CW Communications conferences. Mr. Haugdahl received his B.S. in Computer Science from the University of Minnesota, Institute of Technology.